Pius XII and the Holocaust

Pius XII and the Holocaust
Understanding the Controversy

José M. Sánchez

The Catholic University of America Press
Washington, D.C.

The paper used in this publication meets the minimum requirements of
American National Standards for Information Science—Permanence of
Paper for Printed Library materials, ANSI Z39.48-1984.
∞

LIBRARY OF CONGRESS CATALOGING-IN-PUBLICATION DATA
Sánchez, José M. (José Mariano), 1932–
    Pius XII and the Holocaust : understanding the controversy / José
M. Sánchez.
        p.   cm.
    Includes bibliographical references and index.
    ISBN 0-8132-1080-1 (cloth : alk. paper) — ISBN 0-8132-1081-X
(pbk. : alk paper)
        1. Pius XII, Pope, 1876–1958—Relations with Jews.   2. Holocaust,
Jewish (1939–1945)   3. Judaism—Relations—Christianity.
4. Catholic Church—Relations—Judaism.   5. Christianity and anti-
semitism—History—20th century.   6. World War, 1939–1945—
Religious aspects—Catholic Church.   I. Title.
    BX1378 .S319 2001
    282' .092—dc21

                                              2001017473

Contents

Preface and Acknowledgments, vii

Introduction, 1

1. A Political Papal Life   14
2. Issues, Sources, and Papal Aims and Means   22
3. What Pius Knew about the Holocaust   42
4. What Pius Said about the War   47
5. An Examination of the Reasons   69
   The Least Likely
6. The Need for Protection of German Catholics   81
7. Vatican Diplomacy Has Always Been Cautious   90
8. A Crisis of Conscience for German Catholics   97
9. Pius Feared Communism More than Nazism   103
10. Pius Wanted to Serve as Mediator in the War   108
11. A Papal Protest Would Have Made Things Worse   114
12. Pope Pius' Personality   121
13. The Effect of a Strong Protest   131
    Virtual History
14. Pius and the Countries of German-Dominated Europe   137
15. Conclusion   172
    A Pathetic and Tremendous Figure

Bibliography, 181

Index, 191

Preface and Acknowledgments

Why another work on Pope Pius XII and the Holocaust? The topic of Pius' alleged silence on the Nazi destruction of the Jews has become so controversial that it has become one of the great historical and moral problems of our time. There have been few objective studies of this contentious subject, and those few that have appeared are ignored or dismissed by those whose prejudices they do not confirm. Popular views, especially those bandied about in the media, tend to be based on emotional responses rather than the facts. Some have come to have a life of their own, regardless of their truth or falsity. Even respected historians repeat the views of those critics or defenders that suit their biases, without attempting to go to the primary documents or without trying to verify controversial statements and comments.

The topic is complex, largely because Pius has become a representative of Catholicism—indeed, of Christianity—and therefore of the entire Christian anti-Semitic tradition that led up to the Holocaust. It has become easy to confuse the issues and to make Pius a scapegoat for the destruction of the European Jews. To make the German people or the Christians of Europe responsible is not as emotionally satisfying as selecting a single man whose compulsive personality lends itself to criticism.

Moreover, much of the investigation of Pius' behavior seems more like a legal procedure than a historical examination. Most writers are concerned with condemning or absolving the Pope. Inevitably, historians who are concerned with simply setting the record straight have of necessity to pit themselves against those who argue polemically. As a result, even those seeking objectivity fall into one camp or another. There does not seem to be any way out of this bind.

I began looking into this problem three years ago, after the release of the 1998 report of the papal Commission for Religious Relations with the Jews, "We Remember: A Reflection on the Shoah." After a year, the controversy raised by the Commission's statement that Pius had been responsible for saving hundreds of thousands of Jews appeared to have died down. Then, the publication of John Cornwell's *Hitler's Pope* in the fall of 1999 re-ignited the dispute. A number of works followed. The Pope's defenders, Margherita Marchione and Ronald Rychlak, wrote books that were well-received in traditionalist Catholic circles. Three scholarly studies, those of Michael Phayer and Susan Zuccotti, both critical of the Pope, and the moderate Giovanni Miccoli, each based on extensive archival research, were published in 2000. Undoubtedly other works will have been published by the time this study appears. In all of these works, and in the accompanying reviews and news items, there does not appear to be a lessening of partisanship.

In trying to come to some conclusion on this contentious subject, it appeared useful to me to examine the writings of the important critics and defenders to see how they handled the documents; also, to observe how writers have used them and each other to argue their positions.

This, I believe, will be a fresh look at the topic. My approach is to examine the rationale for Pius' behavior as explained by the scholars and popular writers, make some judgment as to their use of the sources, offer my own opinions, and let the reader make up his or her own mind. In order to do this, I have had to examine the primary sources, where possible.

My own thinking will be revealed as the subject is discussed and examined. I do not pretend to settle the question. I did not settle it in my own mind after reading all of the authors and sources. I certainly cannot ignore my own subjectivity on this sensitive topic, but I hope that readers will find that I try to be as fair as I can to the authors of the works. I am and have been all my life a practicing Roman Catholic. This does not mean that I venerate all of the popes, living or dead. As an historian, I make a sharp distinction between their spiritual lives and actions and their political ones. They themselves often did not, and that is one of the problems the historian must face. From my reading, Pius XII consistently thought in spiritual terms, but was aware of their political ramifications. He was unable to separate the two, as any person in his position and with his responsibilities would be unable to do.

I would like to thank my colleagues at Saint Louis University, Clarence Miller and Daniel Schlafly, both of whom read my manuscript in the early stages and offered helpful criticism. Clarence Miller especially offered his vast linguistic knowledge to help with the translations and to smooth some of my writing. Frank Coppa of Saint John's University and John Zeender of The Catholic University of America reviewed the manuscript for the Press, and offered sound advice; Professor Coppa was especially helpful, drawing upon his extensive knowledge of the modern papacy. Susan Needham at The Catholic University of America Press did a masterful job of copyediting the manuscript. The Mellon Fund of Saint Louis University provided grants to travel and the time to do research and write this work. Needless to say, the interpretations of this controversial subject are solely mine.

April 2001
St. Louis University

Introduction

At the beginning of the twenty-first century, Pope Pius XII has been dead more than four decades. His tomb, below the main altar of Saint Peter's Basilica in Rome, is the object of veneration by many. The cause of his sainthood continues to be advanced. When he died in October 1958, a generation of Catholics who grew to adulthood during his pontificate could not imagine another pontiff who would not have the lean, ethereal image that Pius projected. The two ubiquitous photographs of Pius—one in profile with hands in pointed prayer, the other taken from behind on the balcony overlooking Saint Peter's square, with hands raised in blessing on the multitude below— seemed to capture the papacy at an eternal moment. Pius was the very image of what a pope should look and act like.

He was universally praised by Catholics and non-Catholics alike, as the spiritual leader not only of Catholics but of Western Civilization itself. His reported visions of Jesus and Mary confirmed that he was a living saint. One distinguished visitor to Rome in 1951 said of him,

This is . . . a Pope who so many of us believe will rank among the greatest. Among the gossipers of Rome he is often described as a priest first and a diplomat afterwards. . . . [The Pope] combines his official work with pastoral work, just as still during his public audience he has been known to go into a corner of the audience hall at a peasant's request and hear his confession. . . . He loves the world as another man may love his only son. The enemies whom his predecessor pursued with vigor, he fights with the weapon of charity. . . . The Pope [saying Mass is] doing what every priest does every day, the servant of the servants of God, and not impossibly, one feels, a saint.

The author of that quotation was Graham Greene, hardly an admirer of any hierarch.[1]

Four years after his death, in the late winter of 1963, that image was tarnished by the German playwright Rolf Hochhuth, who published his play, *Der Stellvertreter (The Deputy)*. The play was performed first in Berlin, and then throughout the world in the following years. Labeled as "the most controversial play of our time" on the dustjacket of the translated volume, the work easily lived up to that billing. Hochhuth created a sensation by charging Pope Pius with violating the moral charge of his high office by not speaking out publicly and forcefully in defense of the Jews against the Nazi machine of destruction in World War II.

It was not, however, *The Deputy* alone that challenged the image of Pius as the perfect pope. Pius' successor, Pope John XXIII, forever changed the image of the papacy simply by his presence; and by convoking the Second Vatican Council, John changed the concept of the papacy as well, doing away with the imperial papacy that had sustained Pius and all of his predecessors since the Middle Ages.

The mood of the 1960s was another reason. Historian John Conway, one of the most perceptive observers of the problem, says that there was a general protest against the "traditional and conservative social patterns of Western Europe"; and furthermore, by 1960 the "full barbarity" of the Holocaust finally be-

1. "The Pope Who Remains a Priest," *Life,* 24 September 1951, 146–62.

came known as the result of the work of Jewish scholars.[2] Blame was in the air.

Hochhuth's challenge raised questions that could not be easily answered, and periodically since the 1960s Pius' role in the Holocaust has been questioned to such an extent and so often that it is not certain that the controversy will ever be settled. His defenders claim that he is the scapegoat for the German Nazis— the real criminals who killed the Jews—and that he has been singled out from the many, the Allied leaders, the International Red Cross, and others who did not help the Jews. They have gone to great lengths to justify Pius' behavior. His detractors proceed from *The Deputy,* repeat Hochhuth's accusations, and add some of their own. The issue pops up over and over again. The words "the silence of Pope Pius" have acquired a life of their own, meaning different things to different critics, sometimes having no connection to Pius at all. The controversy has become a free-for-all for anti-Catholics and Catholic defenders, anticlericals and clericals, libertarians and authoritarians, allowing all to vent their feelings and frustrations regardless of the facts.

In 1983, John Conway, in reviewing the last volume of published Vatican documents on the war, wrote, "Since little new direct information is revealed on the motives of the Pontiff himself, it is improbable that either the Pope's critics or his defenders will have cause to change their minds. . . . The most that can be hoped for with this new documentation is that some of the more extravagant statements on either side will be subjected to the discipline of historical fact."[3] Unfortunately, Conway's wish has not come true. A cursory examination of the literature pub-

---

2. "The Vatican, Germany and the Holocaust," in *Papal Diplomacy in the Modern Age,* ed. P. Kent and J. F. Pollard (Westport, Conn.: Praeger, 1994), 105.

3. "Records and Documents of the Holy See Relating to the Second World War," *Yad Vashem Studies* 15 (1983): 332.

lished in the last decade reveals that not only journalists, but also respected historians, have not changed their opinions of the Pope's behavior. To cite two examples, John Weiss, an academic historian and professor of history at the City University of New York, says that Pius "was pro-Nazi to the end."[4] On the other side, Jesuit Robert Graham, one of the four historians with access to the papal archives and a respected historian of the papacy, is quoted as telling journalists that "if the Nazis had encountered a pope like John XXIII, Good Pope John, they would have won the war! The fact that Hitler lost the war is due in part to the firmness of Pius XII."[5]

The most recent controversy (before the publication of this book) was caused by the publication of John Cornwell's work, *Hitler's Pope: The Secret History of Pius XII.*[6] This attack on Pius, obvious from its title, argues that Pius' entire career as nuncio to Germany, Papal Secretary of State, and Pope, was motivated by a desire to centralize papal power, and that, acting from this motive, he destroyed any possibility of grassroots opposition to the Nazis from the German clergy and laity. Cornwell further charges that Pius was anti-Semitic and therefore not concerned about the destruction of the European Jews.

Cornwell's accusations stirred the debate. Jesuit Peter Gumpel, the priest in charge of investigating Pius as a candidate for sainthood, offered a point-by-point refutation of Cornwell's arguments.[7] Jesuit Pierre Blet, the surviving member of the team of editors of the Holy See's published wartime archives, also rejected Cornwell's arguments.[8] Book reviewers and media com-

---

4. *Ideology of Death* (Chicago: Ivan R. Dee, 1996), 354.

5. Cited in Robert Moynihan, "The Pope Skips a Sentence," *Inside the Vatican,* August–September 1996, 15.

6. New York: Viking Press, 1999.

7. "Cornwell's Pope: A Nasty Caricature of a Noble and Saintly Man," *Zenit News Service,* 16 September 1999.

8. "Vatican Historian Comes to Pius XII's Defense," *National Catholic Reporter,* 22 October 1999, 14.

mentators joined the fray. Those who praised Cornwell were taken by his admission that he was a practicing Catholic and that he had started his investigation with the hope of absolving Pius of guilt but had become "morally shocked" by what he had found. Those who criticized Cornwell pointed to his shoddy documentation, innuendoes, and cleverly phrased non sequiturs.[9] The internet was clogged with superficial comments which revealed that no one's mind was changed by the book.

A year and a half earlier, there had been a controversy concerning the document issued by Pope John Paul II in March 1998. This document, "We Remember: A Reflection on the Shoah," the work of the papal Commission for Religious Relations with the Jews, confessed to the world that "many Christians in countries occupied or ruled by the Nazi powers or their allies were horrified at the disappearance of their Jewish neighbors and yet were not strong enough to raise their voices in protest. For Christians, this heavy burden of conscience of their brothers and sisters during the Second World War must be a call to penitence." At the same time, the authors defended Pius XII, pointing out that "during and after the war, Jewish communities and Jewish leaders expressed their thanks for all that had been done for them, including what Pope Pius XII did personally or though his representatives to save hundreds of thousands of Jewish lives."

This defense, according to the document, was based on the statements of many Jews. The authors cite Joseph Nathan of the Italian Hebrew Commission, who said in September 1945, shortly after the end of the war, "We acknowledge the Supreme Pontiff and the religious men and women who, executing the directives of the Holy Father, recognized the persecuted as their

---

9. Ronald Rychlak, *Hitler, the War and the Pope* (Columbus MS: Genesis Press, 2000), 281–307, offers a thorough examination of Cornwell's use of sources and effectively demolishes his interpretations, revealing Cornwell's inadequacy as an historian.

brothers and, with effort and abnegation, hastened to help us, disregarding the terrible dangers to which they were exposed." They also cite Leo Kubowitzki, Secretary General of the World Jewish Congress and of eighty representatives of Jewish refugees from German concentration camps, who also in 1945, "expressed their great honor at being able to thank the Holy Father personally for his generosity towards those persecuted during the Nazi-Fascist period." Finally, they mention the President of Israel, Golda Meir, who on the death of Pius in 1958 sent a message stating, "When fearful martyrdom came to our people, the voice of the Pope was raised for its victims."[10]

Within a few days after "We Remember: A Reflection on the Shoah" was issued, the voices of critics drowned out any praise for Pius. A double-page spread in the *New York Times Magazine* showed a vintage 1927 photo of Pius when he was papal nuncio to Germany, sweeping along in full diplomatic regalia to a waiting limousine, saluted by chauffeur and armed uniformed soldiers, a cleric at his imperious best.[11] The accompanying article cited Jewish leaders' responses to the Vatican statement. Abraham Foxman, national director of the Anti-Defamation League of B'nai B'rith, said, "If Pius XII had said that [anti-Semitism is a sin], the foundations would have shaken beneath him." Arthur Herzberg, former vice-president of the World Jewish Congress, said that Pope John Paul "knows he's going to get to heaven and his maker is going to ask him, 'What did you do?' And he's going to say . . . 'I atoned for Pius XII.'"[12] Many of the nation's largest newspapers echoed them, criticizing Pius for not speaking out in defense of the Jews.

10. The document is in the *New York Times,* 17 March 1998, 10.

11. Which photograph was used on the dust jacket of Cornwell's *Hitler's Pope.*

12. Both citations in Paul Elie, "John Paul's Jewish Dilemma," *New York Times Magazine,* 26 April 1998, 34–39.

More criticism came from abroad. Ignatz Bubis, president of the Central Committee of Jews in Germany, said that he was "particularly incensed at the assertion" that Pius saved hundreds of thousands of Jews: "The Vatican itself saved maybe a few thousand . . . but more than the numbers it was significant that the Vatican kept its activities secret and did not openly speak out for the saving of Jews during the war when it was most needed." Tullia Zevi, leader of the Roman Jewish community, said that the thanks of Jewish leaders after the war and in 1958 "was an immediate expression of gratitude," but "when the possibility arose for a more profound and vast analysis in the subsequent years, the picture was modified." Yisrael Lau, Israel's chief Ashkenazi Rabbi, said, "To say that Pius XII is not guilty—I can't accept that. He was not actively involved, but he contributed [to the Holocaust] by his passivity. We cannot talk about a full apology without mentioning the guilt of the man who stood on the blood [of the dead] and did not prevent the deaths of innocent people."[13]

Traditional defenders of Pius rallied to his cause. Among the more temperate were Jesuit Pierre Blet[14] and Remi Hoeckman, one of the priests who drafted the Vatican document. Hoeckman said, "We need to respect the decisions [Pius] made before God, in particular historical conditions. It is too easy to say 50 years later what Pius XII should or should not have done. We need to give the rightful space to the honesty and conscience of the man."[15] But other traditional defenders of Pius could not completely defend him. The scholarly Owen Chadwick, longtime

13. All quotations from Lynne Weil et al., "Jewish Reactions Are Cool," *Inside the Vatican,* April 1998, 29.

14. "La leggenda alla prova degli archive: le ricorrenti accuse contro Pio XII," *La Civiltà Cattolica* 3456 (1998): 531–54.

15. Cited in John Thavis, "Pope's Theologian: 'I Am Saddened,'" *Inside the Vatican,* April 1998, 32.

professor of church history at Cambridge University, whose *Britain and the Vatican during the Second World War* has great insight into Pius, said of the Vatican document that Pius "was not quite the right man in the right place," and that his hesitation to issue a clear protest, while based on his diplomatic training, was one of those "moments in history when it is better just to speak without thinking."[16]

It would seem a simple task to determine exactly what the Pope said publicly, and to examine the published diplomatic documents to determine much of what he said privately. Both have been done, but the controversy continues. One problem is determining Pius' rationale for his behavior. Pius was a meticulous man, a scholar who weighed his words carefully. Furthermore, as a diplomat, he knew how important the right wording could be. Unfortunately, this close attention to the written word makes it difficult to get at Pius' inner feeling about the enormous problems that he faced. By training and inclination, there was no room for spontaneity in Pius; we do not know what he really felt.

In trying to get at the root of the problem of the myth and the reality of Pius' alleged silence, let me suggest some of the chief problems that cause much of the controversy.

Before anything else, the term "silence" must be dealt with. Pius was not silent about the war. John Pawlikowski, one of the more careful critics, has said, "We should permanently strike the word 'silence' from all Christian-Jewish conversations about the role of institutional Catholicism during the Holocaust. There is a perfectly legitimate discussion to be pursued about the adequacy and the suppositions of Pius' and the Vatican's approach. But this is an altogether different issue from the charge of basic

16. "Pius XII: The Legends and the Truth," *The Tablet,* 28 March 1998, 401.

'silence.'"[17] The term thus has come to mean specifically the lack of a *clear* statement criticizing the Germans for persecuting the Jews.

Another issue needing clarification is the extent to which Pius is a symbol of Christian anti-Semitism. Eugene J. Fisher, a Holocaust scholar, says that the pope symbolizes "not just the Catholic Church but Christians in general. Hence, what was a failing of the Christian community as a whole is 'given a face,' as it were, of a single figure who does not function in the charge as a real person but as a symbol."[18] The pope as symbol, then, has to be carefully distinguished from Pope Pius as a person. This is not an easy or realistically satisfactory task, for symbolism is inherent in the office of the papacy.

Then there is the question of Pius' understanding of the Holocaust in the context of the war years. Did he differentiate the killing of the Jews from the systematic terror, enslavement, and killing of all defenseless people during World War II? There were as many other defenseless noncombatants killed by the Germans as there were murdered Jews. The Nazi regime killed Poles, Gypsies, Russians, homosexuals, Jehovah's Witnesses, and countless other groups, including some German Catholic priests. And the Soviets killed defenseless people, as did the Western Allies later in the war by their terror bombing.

Pius' critics charge him with silence on the killing of Jews, the only group of people singled out by the Nazi regime for total annihilation. Defenders of Pius argue that the carnage of World War II was so immense that the Pope could hardly distinguish one persecuted group from another, and that he spoke

17. "The Vatican and the Holocaust: Unresolved Issues," in *Jewish-Christian Encounters over the Centuries,* ed. Marvin Perry and Frederick M. Schweitzer (New York: Peter Lang, 1994), 298–99.

18. "Foreword," in *Holocaust Scholars Write to the Vatican,* ed. H. J. Cargas (Westport, Conn.: Greenwood Press, 1998), xv.

out many times against the destruction of the defenseless in unspecific but all-inclusive terms. It appears that much of the controversy stems from these different views of what the Pope perceived and when he did so. These views are, in fact, at the root of the dispute.

Another problem is the time frame within which events took place. How Pius reacted in 1944 when the Holocaust was at its terrible height is different from how he reacted in 1939, when the war had not yet broken out but the Jews were being persecuted in Germany. A reaction toward one event does not necessarily imply a reaction toward another, no matter how similar they might be, when the two events are separated by years. Other factors—the degree of knowledge that the Jews were the targets of total destruction, the international situation, the progress of the war, the different personalities and their changing view of events—all involve a change of perspective that critics and defenders should keep in mind. The German scholar Konrad Repgen says that we look at the Holocaust from the end, the final stage, "but viewing the entire process from its gruesome conclusion makes it difficult for us to comprehend how people actually behaved in its unfolding. . . . Unraveling the course of events in a non-deterministic fashion demands considerable moral and intellectual effort."[19]

A connected question is the context in which Pius spoke. Through his public statements, he protested and criticized, but not by name. He stated at the beginning of his pontificate that he would name no names in order not only to preserve the traditional neutrality of the Holy See but more importantly to maintain the possibility of his mediating the conflict, and he

19. "German Catholicism and the Jews: 1933–1945," in *Judaism and Christianity under the Impact of National Socialism,* ed. Otto Dov Kulka and Paul R. Mendes-Flohr (Jerusalem: The Historical Society of Israel and the Zalman Shazar Center for Jewish History, 1987), 213.

kept that promise. However, a careful examination of the particular wartime events taking place as he spoke at a specific time can give great insight into his words; any references to unnamed nations offending morality or violating the rights of defenseless persons must be considered within the particular chronological context.

Parts of the problem of Pius' statements are his style and language. His style is orotund, convoluted, unspecific, guarded; it does not lend itself to simple, direct statements that could be understood immediately by everyone. Victor Conzemius calls his style "curial: too pontifical, too ponderous, too pompous."[20] But Pius was careful of what he said; every word had a precise meaning. The French ambassador to the Holy See, Wladimir d'Ormesson, said Pius "weighed his words on finely calibrated scales."[21]

Then, too, Pius faced many problems, all of them different, yet all interconnected. Both defenders and detractors frequently are unable to separate the problems, and they assume that Pius' reaction to one is the same as his reaction to another. The moral issues involved in the unprovoked German invasion of Poland in 1939 which began the war were similar to, but different from, those involved in the commission of war crimes, not only by the Germans but by their allies and by the Soviets as well.

Furthermore, a distinction must be made between the silence of Pius and the silence of the Church. Many critics look at the silence of national hierarchies, or of individual priests or bishops, and ascribe that silence to Pius. He was, after all, the critics say, the absolute ruler of the Church and therefore in control of any one of his clergy, no matter how lowly. There is no question that many clerics were silent, and worse, approving of and even

20. "Le Saint-Siège pendant la IIe guerre mondiale," *Miscellanea Historiae Ecclesiasticae* 9 (1984): 473.
21. *De Saint-Pétersbourg à Rome* (Paris: Plon, 1969), 307.

collaborating in the destruction of the Jews, and Pius was faced with the problem of what to do about them. His defenders point out that, despite the claims of the imperial papacy, popes simply do not have that much power and in fact cannot even control the curia to their liking.

Another problem has to do with Pius' character and personality. Looked at from the perspective of half a century, Pius was not an attractive person. His solitary life style—eating alone with only his canaries as companions—his authoritarian pronouncements and the impression he gave of omniscience—he gave speeches and allocutions on every conceivable subject, from agricultural mechanics to space exploration—do not lend themselves to admiration. When he became pope in 1939, the most common comment in the press was that he looked like what a pope should look like: the lean body, the nearly transparent skin, the eyes looking heavenward in the staged photos, the pointed prayer hands, all contributed to this image. Pius became a plaster saint. When Pope John came along and destroyed the imperial papacy, Pius' image naturally suffered. The problem is, to what extent is the criticism of Pius and his alleged silence conditioned by this image of his personality? Would critics have the same criticisms of a smiling and affable pope like John XXIII or John Paul I if either had been pope during World War II and reacted the same way Pius did?

Finally, there is the unanswerable question of what would have happened if Pius had made a clear, unequivocal protest against the destruction of the Jews. Here, the historian has to step outside of reality and venture into the realm of virtual history. There are probabilities but no certainties. It is at this point that the historian, scholar or amateur, can devise any scenario he wishes without fear of contradiction, for who can criticize or defend against an event that never happened?

It is these problems that must concern us as we make our way through the thicket of events, claims, criticisms, defenses, probabilities, possibilities, and personalities to determine the facts, motivations, fears, and hopes that surround the problem of Pope Pius XII and the Holocaust. It would be wise to keep in mind an admonition that Michael Marrus, no partisan of Pius, made in a retrospective analysis of the Nuremberg trials. Modern writers, he says, have "prompted unwarranted moral judgements that apply our standards, our appreciations, our sensibilities, our knowledge, and our hindsight to the events of half a century ago."[22]

This study of Pius will heed Marrus' admonition and look at the Pope's behavior and motivation in the context of the events as they happened rather than in the abstract. It is only by doing so that we can understand why Pius acted the way he did; it should also help to clarify the meaning of such terms as the "silence" of the Pope and to lay to rest some of the myths that surround the enigma of Pius and the Holocaust.

22. "The Nuremberg Trial: Fifty Years After," *The American Scholar* 66 (Winter 1997): 563.

Chapter 1

A Political Papal Life

A pope is the leader of a religious institution and as such he is charged with the responsibility for the spiritual welfare of the faithful of that institution, a fact often forgotten in the historiographical controversy surrounding Pius. He was an intensely spiritual person. He wrote a number of major encyclicals dealing with spiritual and religious matters. He prayed constantly. Most of his working hours were given over to religious concerns, administering the institution of which he was the ruler. But of course, secular matters impinged on the religious, and it is to these concerns that this study of Pius must address itself.

Eugenio Pacelli was born to be pope and was on the papal fast track even before he was ordained. His grandfather was one of the founders of the Vatican newspaper, *L'Osservatore Romano;* his father worked as a lawyer for the Holy See. The family belonged to the Black Aristocracy, which supported the papacy through the bleakest days of the Roman Question. From the date of his birth, March 2, 1876, he breathed the air of papal politics and Vatican doings.

He was given papal permission to study for the priesthood at home because of his frail health, and he was ordained in 1899. He had a knack for languages and the scholarly life. He was a curate for a few months, and then entered the papal diplomatic service in 1901, a move that marked his shift from a pastoral career to a diplomatic one. When World War I broke out in 1914, Pacelli was placed in charge of one of the papal humanitarian concerns, that of maintaining a registry of prisoners of war and arranging their exchanges.

In 1917 Pope Benedict XV named him nuncio to the Kingdom of Bavaria, in effect the papal representative to the entire German Empire, as there was no nuncio to Prussia. Benedict consecrated him Archbishop of Sardes, a titular see, for the dignity to go with his new diplomatic office. The Pope charged Pacelli with delivering a peace proposal to Kaiser Wilhelm (which neither the Allies nor the Kaiser accepted unconditionally), and for the remaining years of the war Pacelli lived in Munich, pursuing diplomatic business and continuing his humanitarian activities for prisoners and other victims of the war.

When the war ended with German defeat, the chaotic condition of Germany, the Allied occupation of the Rhineland, and the success of the Bolshevik revolution in Russia led to the proclamation of a Soviet Republic in Bavaria in 1919. A rag-tag "Red Army" made up of anarchists, Communists, and proletarian agitators seized control of Munich. A few of these armed soldiers entered the nunciature and demanded the nuncio's property. Allegedly, Pacelli refused and faced them down, giving rise to the legend that this confrontation with German "Reds" was the origin of his lifelong hatred of Communism.

Pacelli was named nuncio to the new German Republic in 1920. The new pope, Pius XI, elected in 1922 after Benedict's death, pursued a policy of negotiating concordats with all possible nations as a means of protecting the Church, and Pacelli stayed in Munich to negotiate a concordat with Bavaria. In 1925 he moved to Berlin. By this time Pacelli had completely mastered the German language and had assembled a German staff that remained with him the rest of his life. These included his housekeeper, Sister Pascalina Lehnert, and his assistant, Jesuit Robert Leiber. This German influence in Pacelli's household and staff, along with Pacelli's lifelong admiration of German culture, contributed to the later criticism that Pacelli as Pope favored the Germans in the war.

As nuncio, Pacelli negotiated a concordat with the Prussian state in 1929. Later that year, he was named a cardinal, returned to Rome, and early in 1930, Pius XI named him Secretary of State of the Holy See. For the next nine years, Pacelli was the Pope's chief advisor and factotum. He carried out Pius' policies, advised him on diplomatic matters, helped write the Pope's encyclicals, and handled most international matters. He continued the papal policy of seeking concordats. In this capacity, he negotiated the Reich Concordat of 1933, the agreement with Hitler's Germany that later became a target of criticism by his detractors.

Even though German affairs remained troublesome for the Pope and his Secretary of State, other countries also presented enormous problems. There was the ongoing struggle with the Mexican government, which had limited the number of clergy in that nation to an absurdly low number, a measure which in turn had provoked a violent rebellion in the name of Christ, to which the government responded with brutal force. Even worse was the Spanish Civil War, which broke out in the summer of 1936. In the space of a few months nearly seven thousand priests, nuns, and monks, along with countless thousands of Catholic laypersons, were killed by anticlerical uncontrollables who flew the red flag in one form or another, thereby adding to the traditional papal fear of Bolshevism.

As for the Germans, in the years following the signing of the concordat of 1933, Pacelli, at the Pope's direction, sent dozens of protests to the German government citing violations of the accord. Early in 1937, Pius XI asked the German cardinals to help him write an encyclical protesting the Nazi government's perse-cution of the Church. This encyclical, *Mit Brennender Sorge*, was issued on Palm Sunday 1937 and was read in all German church-es. It protested the government's violations of the concordat and also condemned the Nazi doctrines of racism and statism.[1]

By the late 1930s Pacelli's anti-Nazi sentiments were well known. So also was he himself. He had attended Eucharistic congresses in Buenos Aires and Budapest. He had traveled throughout Europe and visited the United States as well. He was the best-known cardinal in the world. Pius XI probably sent him on these journeys for precisely that purpose, intimating at least once that he wanted Pacelli to be his successor on the throne of St. Peter.

In February 1939 Pius XI died. In the conclave that followed, Pacelli was elected Pope on the third ballot. He took the name of his predecessor and became Pius XII. Up to this point, and in fact beyond, there is no question that Pacelli was identified as anti-Nazi both by the future Allies and the Axis powers, largely be-cause of his association with his predecessor but also because of a few anti-Nazi statements he had made. The press in London, New York, and Paris hailed his election, expressing confidence that he would support them in the coming battle between democ-racy and fascism. The Nazi press saw him as continuing the con-frontational policy of Pius XI and therefore as unsympathetic to the Nazis. On the other hand, German diplomats at the Vatican were pleased because the new Pope, despite his opposition to Nazism, was a diplomat and had given assurances before the con-clave that he would be open to conciliation with Germany.[2]

1. While many secondary works claim that Pacelli was the author, in fact the encyclical was written by Cardinal Michael Faulhaber, Archbishop of Munich, with some editing by Pacelli. See Angelo Martini, SJ, "Il Cardinale Faulhaber e L'Enciclica 'Mit Brennender Sorge,'" *Archivum Historiae Pontificiae* 2 (1964): 303–20.

2. Owen Chadwick, *Britain and the Vatican during the Second World War* (Cambridge: Cambridge University Press, 1986), 45–49.

In the six months between Pius XII's election on March 2, 1939, and the outbreak of the Second World War on September 1, the new Pope was occupied with trying to prevent the conflict. He proposed a peace plan, offered to mediate the diplomatic efforts to prevent war, and invited all future belligerents, save the Soviets, to a conference at the Vatican. None of his proposals were accepted by all of the powers, and his efforts came to naught.

When the war began, Pius immediately offered his services for mediation, and throughout the entire conflict he never ceased to maintain that offer, a fact that was made abundantly clear to both sides. At the same time, he had to address a number of other problems created by the war.

A major consideration was the question of the morality of the war started by the German invasion of Poland. He was constantly besought by the Allies (Britain, France, and Poland, at first) to condemn the German action. He was also distressed by the Soviet invasion of Poland, which took place two weeks after the German invasion, in accord with the secret clauses of the Soviet-German non-aggression pact of August 1939. Furthermore, his fears of the Soviets grew after their invasion of Finland in November.

During this time, Pius secretly agreed to serve as a conduit and guarantor between anti-Hitler Germans and the British government to arrange a compromise peace. When the negotiations failed, the Pope apparently came to realize how severely he would have compromised the papacy if the secret negotiations had been discovered by Hitler's government, and he observed strict neutrality thereafter.[3]

In 1940, his concern about the morality of war was further

3. See Harold Deutsch, *The Conspiracy against Hitler in the Twilight War* (Minneapolis: University of Minnesota Press, 1968), 120–21, 145.

heightened by the German invasion of Norway and Denmark in April, and the invasion of France and the Low Countries in May. Pius sent sympathetic notes to the rulers of Belgium, the Netherlands, and Luxemburg, commiserating with them on the unprovoked German attack on their nations.

Pius devoted major effort to attempting to keep Italy out of the war, since by virtue of his position as Bishop of Rome and Primate of Italy, his influence was greater there than in other countries. He was unsuccessful; Italy declared war on Britain and France in June 1940. When France fell to the Germans and was divided in two, the puppet Vichy regime, while undertaking the task of erasing decades of official anticlericalism, joined the other German satellite states in beginning to persecute Jews.

Along with the persecution of the Jews, by the end of 1940, another problem had arisen: war crimes. These included killing of civilians, mistreatment of prisoners of war, and terror-bombing of cities. For Pius, these crimes were not only a matter of great anxiety; they also put a greater demand upon the traditional humanitarian work of the Holy See for the victims of war.[4] These humanitarian activities continued on to the end of the war, as the casualties grew ever larger.

In 1941, the Germans and their allies invaded Yugoslavia and Greece. The Yugoslav state was shattered into its constituent ethnic nations. In the newly independent Catholic Croatia, the fascist Ustasha began a wholesale persecution of Orthodox Serbs, Jews, and Gypsies; many of the Serbs were forced to choose between conversion to Roman Catholicism or death, and others were simply killed. Pius had to deal with the Ustasha leader,

4. During the entire war, Pius was lauded by the press in the United States and Britain for his concern for the victims of war. At the end of 1939, the United Jewish Appeal sent $125,000 to the Pope for aid for refugees. *Actes et Documents du Saint Siège relatifs à la Seconde Guerre mondiale,* vol. 6 (Vatican City: Libreria Editrice Vaticana, 1965–1981), 211–14.

Ante Pavelic, who wanted papal recognition and blessing of his new state. The Pope gave neither, but neither did he condemn the conversions publicly, preferring to work diplomatically to lessen the Ustasha terror.

Then, in June 1941, the Germans invaded the Soviet Union. Some Germans sought Pius' support for this Eastern war, arguing that the German invasion was a crusade against godless Bolshevism. Pius declined to give it. As reports came in to the Vatican of large numbers of Jews being killed in the occupied areas of the Soviet Union, the Pope told his confidantes and diplomats in the Vatican of his anxiety over these atrocities. By the end of 1941, the Germans had been stopped outside of Moscow and the United States had entered the war.

In 1942, the Nazi leaders held the Wannsee conference, at which they decided upon a more systematic killing of the Jews under their control, and the machinery for constructing the death camps, primarily in occupied Poland, was set in motion. By midsummer, the news had been reported to the Pope that Jews were being killed in large numbers. Papal nuncios in the Axis satellite and puppet states reported that governments there were being pressured by the Germans to transport their native and immigrant Jews to Poland for "resettlement." Papal nuncios sought to stop these deportations by diplomatic protest, to little avail in some nations, with greater success in others.

Early in 1943, the Allied leaders at the Casablanca conference issued a statement calling for the unconditional surrender of the Axis powers. Pius was concerned, because he believed that this demand would prolong the war. He was also increasingly alarmed about Allied bombing of German cities. His most pressing problem, however, was the German occupation of Italy, and most particularly Rome, after Italy surrendered to the Allies in September. The German occupation of Rome lasted from September 1943 until June 1944, and for much of northern Italy,

German control lasted until the end of the war. The Vatican came under German surveillance, although German soldiers were forbidden to enter the Vatican. Meanwhile Italian Jews were transported to the death camps.

As Allied armies closed in on Rome in 1944, Pius feared damage to the Benedictine Abbey of Monte Cassino and to Rome itself, as Allied bombs fell on parts of the city near the rail yards. He pleaded with the Allies to spare Rome because of its architectural treasures, and the Romans came to view him as the defender of the city. When Rome was liberated, Pius blessed the Allied forces and granted numerous audiences for the troops.

The war ended in 1945, and Pius immediately took on the mantle of opposition to the Communists in the Cold War. In 1949 he decreed excommunication for Catholics who joined the Communist Party, and he forbade Italian Catholics under pain of excommunication to vote for the Communist slate in the 1948 elections. He was concerned about the Communist purges in the Soviet satellite states, especially by the trials of Cardinals Stefan Wyszynski of Poland, Alojzije Stepinac of Yugoslavia, Josef Beran of Czechoslovakia, and Josef Mindszenty of Hungary, each imprisoned by the Communist regimes in their countries. He forcefully condemned the Soviet crushing of the Hungarian uprising in October 1956.

Pope Pius died in October 1958. The press carried messages of condolence from throughout the world, and he was lauded for his humanitarian activities during the Second World War, not least by Jewish leaders, who specifically cited his protection of Jews from the Holocaust.

Chapter 2

Issues, Sources, and Papal Aims and Means

The Critical Issues

The critics of Pius' behavior have cited a number of issues that they claim prove that Pius was either a moral coward or in favor of a Nazi victory. While the fact that Pius did not issue a clear specific protest against the killing of the Jews remains the paramount charge, these other issues, they argue, support their allegations.

The first of these issues is his negotiation of the German concordat of 1933 when, as Cardinal Pacelli, he was the Secretary of State of the Holy See. Critics argue that he conspired to demolish the German Catholic Center Party in order to get the concordat, thereby destroying a powerful political party that could have blocked Hitler's destructive moves; they argue furthermore that the concordat legitimized Hitler's regime in the eyes of Catholics, not only in Germany, but throughout the world.

Another criticism is that Pius generally favored Germany and the Germans because of his long stay in that country as nuncio from 1917 to 1930. They point to his

Germanic household staff and advisors; his singling out Hitler to give special diplomatic notification of his election as Pope in March 1939, claiming that this was a sign of the new Pope's favor; his urging the Poles to accede to Hitler's demands in the summer of 1939 in order to prevent war, when it was obvious that the German aims were so unjust that it was immoral to give in to them.

The Pope is criticized for continuing to favor the Germans after the war broke out by not protesting the immorality of their attack on Poland and later on the Western countries, and by sympathizing with the German bishops over the Allied bombing of Germany, but not with the British bishops over the bombing of Britain.

Pius is criticized for not condemning the French anti-Semitic laws decreed by the puppet Vichy regime in France. The critics cite French Ambassador Léon Bérard's report to Marshal Pétain that the Vatican had no objection to the anti-Semitic legislation as long as certain Church rights were observed (regarding marriage) and that the laws were carried out humanely.

Another key criticism has to do with the Pope's relations with the leader of the new Croatian state, Ante Pavelic. The critics allege that the Pope supported the Croatian dictator in his persecution of the Orthodox Serbs and Jews because Pavelic established a Catholic state which gave the Church rights long denied by the Serb-dominated Yugoslav state. Some critics claim that the papal nuncios in Slovakia and Hungary could have done more to help the Jews, but the major criticism concerning Slovakia is that the leader of the government was a priest, Josef Tiso, and that the Pope could have excommunicated him or at least disciplined him in some way. As for Hungary, the Pope could have urged the clergy to greater opposition to the deportation of Jews.

One of the most critical issues is the Roman *razzia* (roundup) of the Roman Jews for deportation in October 1943 when Rome was under German occupation. Pius, they claim, could have blocked the move by a protest. Critics further contend that Pius did not order the Italian clergy to provide refuge to the Jews, that what aid was given was done without Vatican approval.

Underlying all criticism is the relationship of Pius with the German bishops. Critics say that Pius was too soft in his dealings with them; that he should have insisted that they oppose the immorality of the Nazi regime, and that he should have used his ecclesiastical power against those bishops who supported the regime.

Furthermore, as proof of Pius' pro-Nazi feelings, critics point to the "rat line," the Vatican's alleged surreptitious support of fleeing Nazi and other Axis war criminals after the war. This support, they claim, enabled those criminals to escape justice. Finally, critics argue that Pius' outspoken criticism of Communists after the war, especially his threatened excommunication of Italian Catholics who supported the Communists in the elections of 1948, proves that he could have used similar measures against the Nazis during the war and that he did not do so because he considered Communism a greater threat than Nazism.

It is all of these accusations, both individually and together, that have led Pius' critics to charge that he deliberately chose not to issue a strong protest against the German destruction of the European Jews. The charges add up to a powerful indictment of Vatican policy and are the basis of the contentious issue of Pius and the Holocaust.

The Deputy

Although German playwright Rolf Hochhuth's *The Deputy* is the most famous indictment of Pius, it was not the first. Five years after the war ended and long before Pius died, Léon Poliakov wrote an article in which he pointed to the Vatican's tacit approval of Vichy France's anti-Semitic laws and said that Pius XII was "less forthright" than Pius XI, postulating "excessive prudence," or the "expectation that Hitler might defeat Moscow," or Pius XII's "supposed 'Germanophilia'" as causes. Poliakov however, praised Pius for helping Jews "by a thousand different means."[1]

Hochhuth's play, however, captured the world's attention,[2] and so powerful was his dramatic skill, and so searing his indictment, that despite criticism which destroyed much of the factual basis of his argument, it has remained the key criticism of the Pope. Hochhuth dedicated his play to two Catholic martyrs of the Nazis: Maximilian Kolbe, a Polish Franciscan who died in Auschwitz after voluntarily taking the place of another prisoner who was selected for retribution punishment following an escape; and Dean (Propst) Bernhard Lichtenberg of St. Hedwig's Cathedral in Berlin, who denounced the persecution of the Jews from the pulpit, was arrested, and died on his way to a concentration camp.

In the play, through his characters and characterizations, Hochhuth makes a number of accusations. In Act I, one of his characters argues that Pius should have unilaterally abrogated the Reich Concordat of 1933 as a protest against the Nazi government's unchristian behavior. In that act Hochhuth introduces a cold-hearted Catholic industrialist (and in his stage directions he has the same actor play the role of Pius as well) who defends arms manufacturer Krupp for beating slave laborers and says that Pius, "by his wise conduct has spared me the necessity of being a bad German" (p. 55). The point is made throughout that any papal action is to be greatly feared by the Nazis.

1. "The Vatican and the 'Jewish Question': The Record of the Hitler Period—and After," *Commentary* 10 (November 1950): 439–49.
2. *The Deputy,* trans. Richard and Clara Winston (New York: Grove, 1964).

In Act II, two points are made: that Hitler fears the Pope more than he fears anyone else, and that Pius has business interests that preclude any condemnation of Germany. Furthermore, a cardinal who presumably has the ear of the Pope argues that Hitler is at last uniting Europe in opposition to the Russians, who want Europe to be under the Orthodox heel. In response to the cardinal who says that a papal threat would only make things worse for the Jews, the priest-protagonist, Riccardo Fontana (who, at the end of the play puts on a yellow star and goes off with the deportees to die at Auschwitz), asks, what could be worse than what is happening to Jews now?

In Act III, which takes place on October 16, 1943, with Rome under German occupation, the stage directions make the point that the roundup of Rome's Jews is taking place "under the Pope's windows"—this taken from Ambassador Ernst von Weizsäcker's actual report to Berlin. Fontana says, "Doing nothing is as bad as taking part" in killing of Jews. "God can forgive a hangman for such work, but not a priest, not the Pope!" (p. 155). And when Germans begin to round up Jews, a sadistic German officer assures a Jew that nothing bad will happen to him because how could the Pope "give such friendly audiences to thousands of members of the German army?" (p. 181).

Act IV is the most revealing. It takes place in the papal apartments. The Pope is characterized as having a "cold, smiling face," "aristocratic coldness," and an "icy glint [to] his eyes" (p. 195). He is concerned about the Vatican's stocks and securities and about the Allied bombing of Italy's factories. He equivocates about his concern for Vatican investment in the factories by saying that the bombings will reduce workers to greater poverty and they will become anarchists. Pius refers to the German deportation of Jews as "tactless" and "extremely bad behavior" (p. 198). Upset at the rumor that he had threatened the Germans with a protest if they did not stop, he says "Whoever wants to help [the Jews] must not provoke Hitler," and, "We have hidden hundreds of Jews in Rome; ... If we keep silent ... We do so also *ad maioram* [sic] *mala vitanda* [to avoid greater evil]" (p. 200).

Then Fontana asks the Pope why he has not made a protest. Pius answers heatedly that he was prepared to pay ransom for the Roman Jews, and that the monasteries are open for the Jews. Then he says that "disaster looms for Christian Europe" (p. 205) and if Hitler is overthrown, Stalin will take over; thus Hitler is the bulwark of Europe. The Pope talks in geopolitical terms of the need to have a strong state in central Europe to keep out the Soviets.

Then, in response to continued pleas for a protest, Pius dictates a typically obtuse papal statement that says little directly; at the same time he tells his financial advisor to look out for Vatican investments in Hungary. He refuses to write to Hitler, saying that he wants to remain impartial.

Act V takes place in Auschwitz and is concerned with the question of how God can allow the Holocaust to take place. The play closes with a quotation from German Ambassador Weizsäcker's letter to Berlin pointing out that the Pope has not protested the deportation of the Jews, and that "since further action on the Jewish problem is probably not to be expected here in Rome, it may be assumed that this question, so troublesome to German-Vatican relations, has been disposed of" (p. 284).

Hochhuth added an appendix entitled "Sidelights on History" to the text of his play. In this he defends himself against the critics of his work. As for documentation, he states that he "examined those memoirs, biographies, diaries, letters, records of conversations and minutes of court proceedings which bear on the subject and which have already been made available." As for a list of what these are, he says, "no bibliography of these well-known sources is needed." Some are mentioned in the context of his defense, but there are quotations and statements that have no citation. As for his method, Hochhuth says, "I allowed my imagination free play only to the extent that I had to transform the existing raw material of history into drama" (p. 287).

Papal defenders have taken Hochhuth to task over his portrayal of Pius and also over the defense of his view in his appendix. And while many of the Pope's critics agree that Hochhuth's pope is a caricature, they still argue that Hochhuth's main point is valid, namely that a papal protest would have had an enormous effect upon Hitler and would have saved many Jews from the fate that Hitler had planned for them.

The Sources

Almost everything that Pope Pius XII said in public in his life has been documented in collections of encyclicals, messages, addresses, and other discourses. Pius was a prolific writer and speaker. He gave addresses to all sorts of groups visiting the Vatican over the nineteen years of his pontificate in addition to writing on a vast range of topics.

From 1939 to 1945, his public statements bearing on the war were his one encyclical, *Summi Pontificatus* (1939), his Christmas addresses to the world, his occasional addresses to the College of Cardinals, and other brief statements to groups visiting the Vatican. He spoke to groups of Axis soldiers while Rome was under Mussolini's control, but there is no record of what he said, and he spoke to Allied soldiers after Rome was liberated in June 1944; his words to them were innocuous.

Another set of sources is the diplomatic papers in the various archives of the countries which had diplomatic relations with the Holy See. No complete set has been published by any country, but there are works which contain some of these documents.

The Holy See adheres to a seventy-five-year rule for opening its archives, so they are not yet open for the wartime period.

However, in response to the clamor set up by Hochhuth's play, in 1964 Pope Paul VI authorized the publication of selected documents by a team of four Jesuits. These historians, Pierre Blet, Angelo Martini, Burkhart Schneider, and Robert Graham (a Frenchman, an Italian, a German, and an American) were the only ones allowed into the archives, but they have given assurances that the published documents faithfully represent the vast archival collection that was not published, and they say that only the constraints of size prevented them from publishing everything, and that there were no secrets that would be revealed in future years when other historians are allowed into the archives.[3]

The documents, collectively published in 11 volumes from 1965 to 1981 with the title *Actes et Documents du Saint Siège relatifs à la Seconde Guerre mondiale*,[4] are all in the original languages, primarily Italian, the working language of the Vatican. In each volume, there is an introduction in French, and each document is headed by a brief description, also in French; each of the volumes is well indexed.

3. See Blet, "La leggenda," 540–41.

4. Vatican City, Libreria Editrice Vaticana, 1965–1981. Hereafter cited as *ADSS*. Volume 1 is entitled *Le Saint Siège et la guerre en Europe, 1939–1940* (1965), and covers the period from the election of Pius XII in March 1939 to August 1940. It is the only volume translated into English, *The Holy See and the War in Europe, 1939–1940* trans. Gerard Noel (London: Herder, 1968, and Washington-Cleveland: Corpus Books, 1968). Volume 2 is entitled *Lettres de Pie XII aux Evêques allemands, 1939–1944* (1967). Volume 3 (in two tomes) is *Le Saint Siège et la situation religieuse en Pologne et dans les Pays Baltes, 1939–1945* (1967). Volume 4 is *Le Saint Siège et la guerre en Europe, Juin 1940–Juin 1941* (1967). Volume 5 is *Le Saint Siège et la Guerre mondiale, Juillet 1941–Octobre 1942* (1969). Volume 6 is *Le Saint Siège et les victimes de la guerre, Mars 1939–Décembre 1940* (1972). Volume 7 is *Le Saint Siège et la guerre mondiale, Novembre 1942–Décembre 1943* (1973). Volume 8 is *Le Saint Siège et les victimes de la guerre, Janvier 1941–Décémbre 1942* (1974). Volume 9 is *Le Saint Siège et les victimes de la guerre, Janvier–Décembre 1943* (1975). Volume 10 is *Le Saint Siège et les victimes de la guerre, Janvier 1944–Juillet 1945* (1980). Volume 11 is *Le Saint Siège et la Guerre mondiale, Janvier 1944–Mai 1945* (1981).

Five of the volumes deal with the war in chronological order. Four are devoted to the humanitarian activities of the Holy See, also chronologically organized. One is the collection of letters between Pius and the German bishops, and one deals with the situation in Poland and the Baltic countries throughout the war. Despite the repeated flare-ups of the controversy and the impassioned comments from detractors and defenders, only one volume has been translated into English, the language of many of Pius' critics—an indication, I believe, of the generally superficial approach to the problem of Pius and the Holocaust.

The Jesuit editors have written articles based on their research, using the documents they published along with other works to illuminate specific problems. Most of these articles have appeared in the Italian Jesuit monthly, *La Civiltà Cattolica.*[5]

Then there are the memoirs of diplomats at the Vatican. These include those of the French Ambassador up to the defeat of France in 1940, François Charles-Roux;[6] his successor, Wladimir d'Ormesson;[7] and the Polish Ambassador, Kazimierz Papée.[8] German Ambassador Ernst von Weizsäcker's papers have been published[9] and the papers of the British Minister to the Holy See, D'Arcy Osborne, are very adequately handled by Owen Chadwick in *Britain and the Vatican during the Second World War.*

Finally, of great value are the memoirs of intimates of Pius. These include his German Jesuit assistant, Robert Lieber,[10] his

5. Robert Graham has been the most prolific writer; see the bibliography in Giovanni Miccoli, *I dilemmi e i silenzio di Pio XII* (Milan: Rizzoli, 2000), 528.

6. *Huit ans au Vatican, 1932–1940* (Paris: Flammarion, 1947).

7. *De Saint-Pétersbourg à Rome.*

8. *Pius XII a Polska* (Rome: Editrice Studium, 1954).

9. *Die Weizsäcker Papiere,* ed. Leonidas E. Hill (Frankfurt: Allstein, 1974).

10. See his articles in *Stimmen der Zeit,* "Pius XII +," 163 (1958–1959): 81–100; and "Pius XII und die Juden in Rom," 167 (1960–61): 428–36.

assistant Secretary of State, Domenico Tardini,[11] and his house-keeper, Sister Pascalina Lehnert.[12]

The Secondary Works

Such is the controversial nature of the topic that some secondary works provide some amount of primary source material, particularly in their citation of comments made by persons who visited Pius and in whom Pius confided, and in interviews with survivors of the period. There is no way of knowing whether these citations are genuine and well founded or simply invented by the persons or authors. In many of the books the citations do not give the details of the source, and one is left to make a judgment on the basis of external evidence: does it seem logical that Pius would have confided in this person, and if so, does what he says agree with what verifiable sources say, and do the survivors' memories appear to be true descriptions of what happened? All that I can do, therefore, is inform the reader of the source, make a judgment, and leave it up the reader to accept or deny the validity of the source.

The first substantial work to appear was, of course, Rolf Hochhuth's *The Deputy*. The dramatic impact of the play and its controversial statements produced a multitude of responses, both attacking and supporting Hochhuth's interpretation. While many of the responses referred to the dramatic style and impact of the play, others offered factual insights into the problem. Many were collected by Eric Bentley in *The Storm over the Deputy*,[13] and there are some primary sources in these responses. Another valuable

11. *Memories of Pius XII*, trans. Rosemary Goldie (Westminster, Md.: Newman Press, 1961).

12. *Ich durfte ihm dienen: Erinnerungen an Papst Pius XII* (Würzburg: Verlag Johann Wilhelm Naumann, 1982).

13. New York: Grove, 1964.

work in the same vein is Fritz J. Raddatz, ed., *Summa Iniuria oder Durfte der Papst schweigen?*[14]

The first substantive historical work to use unpublished documents was Saul Friedlander, *Pius XII and the Third Reich: A Documentation.*[15] Friedlander, a survivor of the Holocaust and later an academic historian, based his study on German diplomatic documents, chiefly from the embassies at the Holy See and Rome. He uses the documents selectively, seldom giving Pius the benefit of the doubt. Friedlander admits that they give an incomplete picture of the problem and says that a study based on them "cannot but be very biased; it goes without saying that no definite conclusions can be drawn without knowledge of the Vatican documents."[16] Those documents had not been published when he wrote the book; for the English edition, published two years later, he notes that the first volume of the Vatican documents had by that time appeared; "However, what has been published up to now does not, on the whole, seem to contradict in any way the impression given by the documents published in my book, for the same period [March 1939 to August 1940]."[17] A singular problem, which Friedlander admits, is that practically all of his documents are those of German diplomats; he does not explore the veracity of those diplomats and the possibility that they might have been coloring their observations in order to find favor in Berlin, to tell the Foreign Office and the Nazi party leaders what they wanted to hear rather than what the diplomats' genuine views were. Few critics who cite Friedlander in making their judgement take his caveats into consideration; most use his documents without taking into account the Vatican pub-

14. Hamburg: Rowohlt, 1964.
15. Trans. Charles Fullman (New York: Knopf, 1966), from the original, *Pie XII et le IIIe Reich, Documents* (Paris: Éditions du Seul, 1964).
16. Friedlander, *Pius XII*, xvii.
17. Friedlander, *Pius XII*, x.

lished sources. In any event, after citing the German documents, Friedlander concludes that those sources agree that Pius "seems to have had a predilection for Germany which does not appear to have been diminished by the nature of the Nazi regime and which was not disavowed up to 1944" and that Pius "feared a Bolshevization of Europe more than anything else and hoped, it seems, that Hitler Germany, if it were eventually reconciled with the Western Allies, would become the essential rampart against any advance by the Soviet Union toward the West."[18]

Another important work unearthing sources is Carlo Falconi, *The Silence of Pius XII.*[19] A journalist and the author of works on papal history and an enthusiastic account of Pope John XXIII and Vatican Council II, Falconi traveled to Poland and Croatia to find documents concerned with Pius' relations with those two areas. In Poland, most of the sources came from clandestine underground groups; in Zagreb, the sources were from the Croatian government's representatives at the Vatican in 1942 and 1943. Falconi thus places emphasis on these two areas which had not been investigated in any detail before. His conclusion is that Pius "did not dare to adopt a decisive position against the civilian misdeeds of the Nazis and their allies—in spite of ardently wishing to do so," and "the fact that, in my belief, Pius XII was silent not out of fear, but for respectable if inadequate motives, means that we cannot brand him with infamy, even if it does not absolve him from undoubted responsibility. In any case, a severe judgment on his silence does not exclude an open-minded and

18. Friedlander, *Pius XII*, 236. John Conway, *The Nazi Persecution of the Churches* (New York: Basic Books, 1968), 450, says of Friedlander: "He has chosen to overlook the most significant of the Papal protests, which, despite his contention, are to be found in the sources he has used. This arbitrariness in selection is matched by a bias in interpretation which extends even to the translations in the various editions of his book."

19. Trans. Bernard Wall (Boston: Little, Brown, 1970), from the original, *Il silenzio di Pio XII* (Milano: Sugar Editore, 1965).

unconditional recognition of all that he did to prevent the outbreak of war, to discourage its spreading, and to alleviate the
sufferings of its victims."[20] But despite this disclaimer, Falconi,
like Friedlander, when he examines the individual charges, does
not give Pius the benefit of the doubt.

More recently, Pierre Blet, one of the Jesuit editors of the
Vatican documents, has written *Pie XII et la Seconde Guerre mondiale d'après les archives du Vatican*, a narrative analysis of Pius' and
the Vatican's activities during the war based largely on the Vatican documents; while favorable to the Pope, it is the first work
to attempt an overall study of papal policy with all the warring
nations during the war. Unfortunately it lacks the specific citations for the many documents on which Blet bases his argument.[21]

British journalist John Cornwell's *Hitler's Pope* (1999) is partly
based on his reading of unpublished documents of testimonies
for the beatification process of Pius, along with some documents from Pacelli's years as nuncio to Bavaria that had recently
been opened in the Vatican State Secretary archives under the
seventy-five year rule. However, Cornwell has used the beatification documents selectively to argue his sensational thesis, and
the texts of some of the nunciature documents had already been
printed in Emma Fattorini, *Germania e Santa Sede: Le nunziature de
Pacelli tra la Grande guerra e la Reppublica di Weimar.*[22]

Three recent works based on extensive archival research are
Michael Phayer, *The Catholic Church and the Holocaust, 1930–
1965,*[23] Susan Zuccotti, *Under His Very Windows: The Vatican and*

20. Falconi, *Silence*, 15.

21. Paris: Perrin, 1996. There is an English translation by Lawrence J.
Johnson, *Pius XII and the Second World War according to the Archives of the Vatican* (New York: Paulist Press, 1999).

22. Bologna: Società editrice il Mulino, 1992.

23. Bloomington: Indiana University Press, 2000.

the Holocaust in Italy,[24] and Giovanni Miccoli, *I dilemmi e i silenzio di Pio XII.* Phayer is critical of Pius, putting the Pope's behavior in the larger context of the actions of those clergy and laity who persecuted and of those who aided the European Jews; and he takes his theme through the Cold War as well. Zuccotti is also critical of the Pope, contending that his alleged support of the Italian Jews is largely a myth; her research is based on a close reading of the Vatican documents and interviews with survivors. Miccoli, an Italian scholar, draws upon vast bibliographical reading to argue that the Vatican's machinery of protest was anachronistic and more suited to the religious wars of the Middle Ages in being general rather than specific.

Among other secondary works of value is Guenter Lewy, *The Catholic Church and Nazi Germany,*[25] somewhat critical of Pius, but concentrating more on the German bishops and their relations with the Nazi regime; Lewy, a political scientist at the University of Massachusetts, was the first to publish a work in English based on extensive archival research into Church documents in Germany.[26] Other useful studies include the early work of Alberto Giovannetti, *L'Action du Vatican pour la paix (Documents inédits: 1939–1940);*[27] the two works by Giorgio Angelozzi Gariboldi, *Pio XII, Hitler e Mussolini,*[28] and *Il Vaticano nella Seconda Guerra Mondiale;*[29] the books of Jacques Nobécourt, *"Le Vicaire"*

24. New Haven: Yale University Press, 2000.

25. New York: McGraw-Hill, 1964.

26. Other documents on the German Church and the Vatican during the years that Pacelli was the Secretary of State can be found in Repgen, "German Catholicism"; Ludwig Volk, *Kirchliche Akten über die Reichskonkordatsverhandlugen 1933* (Mainz: Matthias Grunewald Verlag, 1969); Klaus Scholder, *The Churches and the Third Reich,* trans. John Bowden (Philadelphia: Fortress Press, 1988); and Heinz Hurten, *Deutsche Katholiken, 1918–1945* (Paderborn: F. Schöningh, 1992).

27. Trans. E. de Pirey (Paris: Fleurus, 1963).

28. Milan: Mursia, 1988.

29. Milan: Mursia, 1992.

et l'Histoire,[30] and Léon Papeleux, *Les silences de Pie XII;*[31] the many fine articles by John Conway;[32] Victor Conzemius, "Le Saint-Siège pendant la IIe guerre mondiale,"[33] one of the best brief treatments of the topic; and finally the collection in Michael R. Marrus, ed., *The Nazi Holocaust.* Vol. 8.3: *Bystanders to the Holocaust.*[34]

Papal Aims and Means

In reading the literature on the controversy, one problem becomes immediately apparent: confusion over the aims and means of the papacy. What were the Pope's aims? How did he intend to carry them out? What means were available to him? What did he himself have to say about those aims and means?

There is even confusion over a pope's first obligation. As head of an institutional church, he is charged with protecting that church; according to Catholic theology, the Church is the necessary means of providing the sacraments which give the grace needed for salvation. Without the priests to administer the sacraments and the freedom to receive them, Catholics can be hindered in their search for salvation. Whatever the political situation in a country, the need for priests to administer the sacraments must be one of most important concerns of the pope. While Susan Zuccotti says that placing providing the sacraments above concern for Jewish lives was "a harsh doctrine with harsh consequences,"[35] Giovanni Miccoli, the prolific Italian Holocaust schol-

---

30. Paris: Editions du Seuil, 1964.

31. Brussels: Vokaer, 1980.

32. See especially, "The Vatican, Germany and the Holocaust."

33. *Miscellanea Historiae Ecclesiasticae* 9 (1984): 451–75.

34. Westport, Conn.: Meckler, 1989. There is an excellent bibliographical article (to 1968) by Danilo Veneruso, "Pio XII e la Seconda Guerra Mondiale," *Revista di storia della chiesa in Italia* 22 (1968): 506–53.

35. Zuccotti, 316.

ar, points out that "it is amazing how difficult it is for people to understand that the Church's main aim is to save souls."[36] Historian Beate Ruhm von Oppen argues the point well: she says that Bernhard Lichtenberg of Berlin, who was imprisoned and sent to Dachau for his sermons against the regime's killing of Jews, "was driven to panic only once—when he thought he would die in jail without a priest [to administer the last sacraments]."[37] Robert Graham, the American Jesuit who edited the Vatican documents, says that a pope's first duty is to support the bishops in their apostolic ministry.[38]

Another papal obligation has to do with his position as Vicar of Christ. In this role he has to take the place of Christ in this world and do the things that Christ would do. This implies denouncing injustice. It also means making people—not just Catholics—aware of their obligations to God and to other people, specifically by obedience to the natural law and to divine law, and to Christ's admonition to love God and to love one's neighbor as oneself.

Ideally these two aims should not conflict with one another. But when they do, which should take precedence? The aim that has the best chance of succeeding or the one that appears more morally defensible? To put it in terms of the actual conflict that Pius faced, should he have protected Catholics, particularly those under Nazi control in Germany and the satellite states, by doing nothing to antagonize the Nazi regime in order to avoid any reprisals against them; or should he have denounced the Nazi regime for its inhumanity to all people? And would the

36. Miccoli, *I dilemmi*, 409.

37. Nazis and Christians," *World Politics* 21, no. 3 (1969): 395.

38. *The Pope and Poland in World War II* (London: Veritas, n.d.), 13. One of the chief arguments of Michael Phayer, *The Catholic Church*, 109, is precisely this: that Pius failed to direct and then support a protest of the Holocaust by the bishops.

powerful Nazi regime have paid any attention to his protest? Obviously the second option is the more morally defensible, but the first option had the better chance of succeeding. This was the dilemma Pius faced.

There are few historians who would disagree with the assertion that World War II was not just a war of arms, but also a war of morality. The Nazi regime was evil; few comparisons can be found in recorded history. The Pope therefore had to play a major role in this conflict because he represented Christian morality. In these unique circumstances, his obligation and his opportunity to protect the Church and Catholics from this evil conflicted directly with his obligation and lack of opportunity to protect all of humanity from the same evil. Hence the dilemma.

This dilemma was compounded by the geographical existence of the Vatican in Fascist Italy. In the Lateran Accords that ended the Roman Question and provided for mutual recognition between the Italian state and the Holy See, the Holy See promised to maintain neutrality in conflicts between states, at the same time reserving to itself the prerogative and obligation to speak out on moral questions—another dilemma in itself.[39]

What did Pius himself believe his aim to be? In receiving the credentials of the Belgian Ambassador to the Holy See two weeks after the war began, he recounted his efforts to prevent the outbreak of war, and then said he now wanted to use his best efforts toward concluding an honorable peace, and at the same time to "ease the terrible injuries already inflicted or those which will be inflicted in the future." He specifically referred to the public affirmation by the belligerent powers that they intended to observe the "laws of humanity in the conduct of the war," and that therefore he hoped that civilian "life, property,

39. See the interesting and prophetic article by Giorgio La Pira, "The Political Heritage of Pius XII," *Foreign Affairs* 18 (April 1940): 486–506.

honor and religious sentiments . . . will be respected," and that prisoners of war "will be treated humanely."[40]

How did he intend to do this? According to the editors of the Vatican documents, by "instruction and reminders of Christian doctrine, either by public solemn messages, or by exhortations and direct admonitions to the clergy and to the faithful of the Church and to responsible authorities and finally by diplomatic action in all forms consistent with the international position of the Holy See."[41] According to this view, no papal protest or threat was precluded; only diplomatic action appeared to be circumscribed by some restraint.

What means were available to the Pope? A simple protest would be to state that killing and/or abusing defenseless people is wrong, without naming offenders or places. As shall be seen, he did this in his Christmas message of 1939, shortly after the war broke out. He labeled crimes against defenseless persons as crimes that cry out to God for vengeance. This would appear to qualify as a simple protest free of much papal rhetoric.

A second kind of protest would be to state that killing and/or abusing Jews is wrong. In his 1942 Christmas message, he came close to doing so, but he did not mention Jews by name, and his rhetoric is anything but simple. He said that the "magnanimous and upright" should make a solemn vow to reestablish a just society. "Mankind owes that vow" to the dead in battle, to the civilians who have been hurt by the war, and "Mankind owes that vow to the hundreds of thousands of persons who, without any fault on their part, sometimes only because of their nationality or race, have been consigned to death or to a slow decline."[42]

Another protest would be to state in more detail the crime and the punishment involved. For example he could state that

40. 14 September 1939, *ADSS* 1:284–87.

41. *ADSS* 1:vii.

42. *The Catholic Mind* 40 (January 1943): 41–60.

killing and/or abusing defenseless persons, specifically Jews, was a grievous sin, from which a Catholic could be absolved only by his confessor. Pius did not make such a statement.

Another, and more serious form of protest would be to excommunicate persons guilty of crimes against the defenseless. But, excommunications in such broad terms in the circumstances of modern wars are difficult to administer. Does the soldier who kills civilians while attempting to gain a military objective merit this punishment? Moreover, only in a totally Catholic society which accepts the concept of excommunication does such a punishment work. Neither Germany nor any of the states under its control or allied with it was totally Catholic; would even those with a substantial majority of Catholics be swayed by the threat of clerical punishment? Years of papal and clerical threats against anticlerical legislation in countries such as Italy had proved the futility of such threats. Furthermore, the coercive power of the modern secular state is great, and few believers can make the choice to obey the Church against the state, as witness the scant number of German Catholics who heard Pius XI's denunciation of Nazi racism and who publicly opposed the persecution of the Jews and other innocents. Excommunication as used in the distant past was primarily against monarchs to bring them to heel, because excommunication of a ruler absolved his subjects from obeying him. Would such a threat work against a modern leader like Hitler who was a baptized Catholic, but had long since left the Church, even though he kept his name on the tax rolls in Germany as a Catholic? Would German Catholics refuse to follow an excommunicate?

One of the most effective protests would be an interdict, the suspension of religious services in a particular area. The rationale behind an interdict is that the people would put pressure on the leaders because they would want their religious services back. Under an interdict, no masses could be said, no sacraments could be administered, the dead could not be buried with any sort of service, nor could children be baptized. Would Hitler have been open to such pressure from Catholics?

Another papal action could have been directing the clergy to instruct the faithful to help the Jews. Historian Michael Phayer says, "even without a public protest, [Pius] could have communicated with church leaders throughout Europe, admonishing those who disdained the Jewish people and encouraging all of them to urge Catholics to provide shelter for Jews. The consequence would have been fewer Catholic collaborators and bystanders, on the one hand, and more Catholic rescuers and fewer victims on the other."[43] Susan Zuccotti agrees with Phayer and argues further that a protest would have alerted Jews to the nature of the German destructive machinery in a way that no other leader's warning would have done.[44]

In his first encyclical, *Summi Pontificatus*, a month and a half after the war began, Pius talked of his responsibility "to testify to the truth," and said "in the fulfillment of this duty, we shall not let ourselves be influenced by earthly considerations."[45] In fact, earthly considerations became a very powerful influence on Pius. And this fact becomes a large part of the problem of Pius and the Holocaust. His critics argue that he did not "testify to the truth" with sufficient vigor to have an effect, and that "earthly considerations" included venal, petty, and self-serving considerations. His defenders say that he did speak out, but that given the power of the Nazi state, little could be achieved, and that in private the Pope did a great deal to lessen the terror against *all* victims of Nazism.

It is these issues that this study will examine.

43. Phayer, *Catholic Church*, 217.
44. Zuccotti, 310
45. *The Catholic Mind* 37 (8 November 1939): 890–918, paragraphs 19 and 20.

Chapter 3

What Pius Knew about the Holocaust

An important question that influences both criticism and defense of Pius is, how much did he know about the Nazi killing of the Jews and when did he first find out about the systematic mass killings in the death camps? It is not a simple question, for, if he did not know, then he could not protest; and if he did know, how much did he know and when? Furthermore, a distinction must be made between the nonlethal and random persecution of the Jews and the systematic mass killings. Like everyone else in Europe, Pius knew that the Nazis were persecuting Jews and had been doing so since Hitler came to power in 1933. He had helped edit Pius XI's protest of German racism in *Mit Brennender Sorge* in 1937. After he became pope and the war began, the persecution stepped up when the Germans occupied Poland with its large Jewish population. Pius got news of that continuing persecution. Throughout 1940, decrees and legislation in the occupied countries deprived Jews of their legal rights. Forced labor camps for Jews were established in Poland, and Polish Jews were herded into ghettos. Anyone with access to diplomatic information knew that Jews were dying in larger numbers than other victims of Nazi terror, although the Germans had not yet decided upon a course of systematic mass killings. And, however much Pius was concerned about the other victims of German oppression, it must have been obvious to him and to any informed person that the Jews were being singled out for special persecution.

There is no evidence before 1941 that the Germans were planning the mass killing of all Jews.[1] It was not until the invasion of the Soviet Union in the summer of 1941, when they came into control of millions more Jews to add to the millions in Poland already under their domination, that the Germans set up mobile death squads and began to kill hundreds of thousands of Jews.

Some German Jews were transported to the ghettos of Eastern Europe in the fall of 1941. Others were sent to concentration camps. In January 1942, the Germans decided at the Wannsee Conference to regularize the sporadic massacres and to do it more effectively by constructing death camps. Once this was done, throughout the rest of 1942, Jews from the occupied countries of Western Europe were transported to the death camps. This fact became known by the Pope in March 1942 when the nuncios in Slovakia and Switzerland informed the Holy See of the massacres.[2]

But did Pius believe what he was told about the mass killings of Jews? Vatican sources of information were not good, despite the belief of some historians that the Pope, by virtue of what they called his position as absolute monarch of the Church, was privy to all sorts of information, and that the hundreds of thousands of priests in Europe were direct conduits of information

1. Leni Yahil, *The Holocaust: the Fate of European Jewry, 1932–1945* (New York: Oxford University Press, 1990), 253.

2. Walter Laqueur, *The Terrible Secret* (Boston: Little Brown, 1980), 55ff.

to the Pope.[3] Owen Chadwick argues to the contrary, that nuncios were not well informed; that Vatican officials relied upon the British Minister, D'Arcy Osborne, who "spent hours a day listening to the BBC, making summaries of the news reported and getting it into the Italian for the Pope . . . [and] was assured by members of the Vatican staff that this was the only information, or almost the only information, which came to the Pope's eyes from sources which were not under Axis control."[4] Furthermore, the Vatican was rife with rumors, which claimed that the Pope was siding with one side or the other, depending upon the aims of the rumormongers. The Germans, British, and Italians all participated in fabricating these rumors.

To handle all of this information, the staff at the Vatican Secretariat of State numbered only thirty-one, including archival and clerical personnel.[5] Given the abundance of rumors and the paucity of staff, there is then little wonder that the Holy See was cautious in evaluating the information it received. There was a precedent for this caution: in World War I, British propagandists had exaggerated German atrocities in Belgium, concocting fantastic stories about priests being used as bell-clappers and nuns being raped; only after the war had these been found out to be untrue. Ironically, the scale of German terrorism in World War II prompted even greater caution. Even among the Allies and the Jews themselves, the enormity of the German killings could scarcely be believed. It was apparently this fact that kept the pa-

3. Laqueur, *Secret*, 55. Phayer, *Catholic Church*, 43–50, argues likewise, and furthermore condemns the Vatican for not informing the world about the Holocaust.

4. "The Pope and the Jews in 1942," in *Persecution and Toleration*, ed. W. J. Sheils (London: Basil Blackwell, 1984), 436.

5. Further, "the number of papal officials with any access to material on German-Vatican relations would scarcely exceed a dozen": David Alvarez and Robert A. Graham, SJ, *Nothing Sacred: Nazi Espionage against the Vatican, 1939–1945* (London: Frank Cass, 1997), 181, 178.

pal Secretary of State, Luigi Maglione, arguing with other diplomats. He told the American envoy, Harold Tittmann, in October 1942 that the Holy See could not verify the reports of massacres.[6]

Did Pius know that these killings were simply the first step in the German plan to kill all the European Jews? To move from the fact of persecution, to the knowledge that they were killing many, to the belief that they were going to kill all is a big leap. It was not commonly believed by the Allied leaders, who with their espionage services were probably in a better position to know German aims.[7] John Conway says that "it is possible to agree with Owen Chadwick's view that, like the majority of educated men in Western Europe, the Pope could not conceive of iniquity on such a scale, which was a failure of imagination, rather than of nerve."[8] And did Pius feel compelled to make a distinction between the Jews and the other victims of Nazi terror? This is a crucial question, central to the entire argument about his alleged silence.

Susan Zuccotti says that it does not matter that the Pope did not know or understand that the Germans intended to kill all the Jews: "What matters is that the Pope and his diplomatic officials knew enough about the Jewish genocide to believe that it was a disaster of immense, unprecedented proportions. Given what they knew, they should have acted vigorously."[9]

6. Leland Harrison to Cordell Hull, 16 October 1942 in United States Department of State, *Foreign Relations of the United States: Diplomatic Papers 1942* (Washington: United States Government Printing Office, 1961) 3:777. Hereafter cited as *FRUS*.

7. See Michael Marrus, *The Holocaust in History* (Hanover, N.H.: University Press of New England, 1987), 156ff.

8. Conway, "Vatican, Germany and the Holocaust," 114. Miccoli, *I dilemma*, 410, agrees, noting that the Pope could not cope with the terror of modern war because he came from a humane background.

9. Zuccotti, 112.

In any event, it appears that the Pope knew about the massacres by the end of 1942, for he mentioned them, through the thicket of papal rhetoric, in his Christmas message of 1942 and he continued with oblique references in his statements in 1943.

The issue is complicated by the fact of German aggression in the first place. Germany invaded the countries of Europe—a clear act of aggression. Then, the Germans killed millions of noncombatants in the countries they invaded, some by the arguably unavoidable act of military action in civilian areas, but most in cold blood. This was a fact known to the world right from the beginning of the war. The Pope condemned the aggressive power, not by name, but by intimation.

In fact, the distinction between the destruction of the Jews and the destruction of all other innocents is blurred because of the ubiquity of the Nazi aggression. Were the people at the time aware of the distinction? Did the Pope make the distinction, or did he look at the German aggression and their killing of innocents of all kinds, including the Jews, as one horrendous destructive act?

If one sees the Holocaust in the context of the killing of all peoples, not just Jews, then the Pope was aware of it and he consistently condemned it, but not with the language or the force that later critics have demanded. Why he did not issue a forceful protest and a strong condemnation of the German regime is the paramount question of the contentious issue of Pius XII and the Holocaust.

Chapter 4

What Pius Said about the War

Public Addresses

There have been any number of commentaries on Pope Pius' public words on the war, but few have done so in the context of the actual events occurring when he delivered his addresses, encyclicals, and other discourses.

The Pope had moral power, if anyone would respect it. He could condemn the war, and as could be expected, he did; but national policies greatly overrode papal concerns. There is no evidence that any person in political power paid any attention to papal statements, other than giving them lip service when it suited his aims. The Pope's statements were heralded by journalists and clerics, but neither had any influence on wartime activities, and certainly not on ending the war.

From the first weeks of his pontificate, Pius pleaded with the powers to avoid war. But he was most circumspect, not naming names and avoiding any hint that one power was worse than another or that the Germans were bent on unjustified aggression.

Once the war began, he said that he wanted to use his powers to mediate the conflict, and this remained his goal throughout the war. While such an aim may have appeared unrealistic after January 1943 when the Allies announced the doctrine of unconditional surrender, Pius knew that there were Germans anxious to overthrow Hitler and establish a new German government that would repudiate Nazism. He undoubtedly hoped that they would come to him for mediation, and at that point the Allies might lessen their demands. But until that time he had to face the fact that the Nazi leaders did not trust him; he was perceived by them to be so firmly on the side of the Allies that mediation between the Allies and the Nazis was probably impossible. John Conway says, "In reply to those who maintain that the Pope failed in his duty to denounce Nazi crimes and atrocities because of a certain sympathy for Hitler's authoritarian regime, it must be stressed that the Nazi hierarchy in Berlin never regarded the Pope as an ally."[1]

Most of Pius' words are bound up in papal rhetoric and scriptural allusions rather than formulated as direct statements. However, when his few direct statements are looked at in context, it becomes obvious that those he criticized could only be, for the most part, Germany and the Soviet Union.

The Pope set the rules of discourse. He said from the beginning that he was not going to name names, and as far as criticism was concerned, he did not. He did name some names when he mentioned victims and praised those who helped the Holy See.

His first public address after the war began was to the Belgian Ambassador, on September 14, 1939. The Pope expressed his grief about the war and stated his intention to mediate an honorable peace.[2] A few days later, on September 26, 1939, he addressed a group of German pilgrims, telling them that the war

1. *The Nazi Persecution of the Churches,* 239.
2. *ADSS* 1:286.

"is, for all peoples involved in it, a terrible punishment of God," and he hoped for a peace "with honor, with justice, with reconciliation and settlement and which shall also mean happier days and greater freedom again for the Catholic Church in your beloved fatherland."[3]

But more publicity was given to his address to a group of Polish pilgrims led by the Cardinal Primate of Poland, August Hlond on September 30, 1939, shortly after the surrender of the Polish army to Germany. He set the tone of his address by saying, "You have come neither to formulate vindication nor to express loud laments, but to ask from Our heart and lips words of consolation." He consoled the Poles in their suffering, talked of the great deeds of the Poles, and said that God had not forgotten them. The only criticism of Poland's enemies was a statement that "We will also hope (not withstanding many reasons to fear, reasons caused by the too well-known designs of the enemies of God) that Catholic life will be able to carry on."[4] Did enemies of God mean enemies of Poland as well? There were only two enemies of Poland, the occupying powers of Germany and the Soviet Union, which had also invaded Poland.

On October 20, 1939, less than two months after the beginning of the war, Pius issued his first encyclical letter, *Summi Pontificatus*.[5] At the beginning of this letter, Pius said that the first duty of the Pope is to "give testimony to the truth" and that this duty "necessarily entails the exposition and confutation of errors and human faults." He continued: "In the fulfillment of this, Our

3. *ADSS* 1:293.

4. *The Catholic Mind* 37 (22 November 1939): 941–45. *ADSS* has extracts from some of the public statements, but *The Catholic Mind* has complete texts and, along with *The Tablet* and *The New York Times*, is the source most readily available in English. See Chadwick, *Britain and the Vatican*, 81–82, for more on this speech and the Polish reaction.

5. *The Catholic Mind* 37 (8 November 1939): 890–918.

duty, we shall not let Ourselves be influenced by earthly considerations nor be held back by mistrust or opposition, by rebuffs or lack of appreciation of Our words, nor yet by fear of misconceptions and misinterpretations."

The encyclical dealt in generalities: the world is falling into error because it ignores the truths of Christianity as expounded by the Popes. Deification of the State is condemned, so also the neglect of Catholic education of youth. The age is spiritually empty. Specific errors include denial of universal norms of morality, charity, and order. The middle part of the encyclical laid great stress upon equality of all people, the unity of the human race. The state should not break treaties without negotiation and must work for mutual trust among nations. There is a call for more clergy.

At the end of the encyclical, he mentioned the war and said, "The blood of countless human beings, even noncombatants, raises a piteous dirge over a nation such as our dear Poland, which . . . has a right to the generous and brotherly sympathy of the whole world." No other country is mentioned by name in the encyclical (except Italy, which he stated earlier, he is pleased to acknowledge for concluding the Lateran pacts). Again, there were only two nations that could be perceived as persecuting noncombatants at that time: the occupying powers of Germany and the Soviet Union.

The German regime did not allow the publication of this encyclical. Friedlander cites a Gestapo letter that stated, "Readings of the encyclical in the churches are not to be hindered, but that all other forms of circulation, particularly by handbill, are to be stopped [and the Ministry] has prohibited any discussion of the encyclical by the press, including the religious press."[6] The French dropped 88,000 copies of the encyclical on Germany by

6. Friedlander, *Pius XII*, 37.

air. The German newspaper *Deutsche Allegemeine Zeitung*, in com-
menting on the encyclical, said that the Pope's compassion for
Poles should also mention compassion for Germans "who were
the victims of Polish hatred."[7] Furthermore, the Nazi regime did
more than restrict publication for Germans; it changed the language of the encyclical, substituting the name of Germany for
that of Poland, and then distributed copies of this altered document in occupied Poland, so that the Poles reading it would believe that Pius' sympathy was expressed for Germany.[8]

Following this encyclical Pius issued his Christmas message of
December 1939.[9] In this message, he bemoaned the fact of war
and said, "We, the Christian brotherhood, have been obliged, unfortunately, to witness a series of acts incompatible with the rule
of international law, with the principles of natural law and with
the most elementary feelings of humanity."

"In this category fall: the premeditated aggression against a
small industrious and peaceful people, under the pretext of a
threat which was neither existent, desired, nor even possible."
This paragraph applied to the Soviet invasion of Finland, according to *L'Osservatore Romano*,[10] and critics have pointed out
that Pius was willing to condemn the Soviets in unmistakable
terms, but not willing to condemn the German invasion of
Poland as clearly.

Then, he went on to condemn war crimes, again without
naming countries: "Atrocities and illicit use of means of destruction even against noncombatants and refugees, against old
people, women and children [and] the contempt of dignity, freedom and human life, [are] actions that call for vengeance in the
sight of God." He did point out that "although up to now—

7. *The Tablet*, 18 November 1939, 582.
8. Chadwick, *Britain and the Vatican*, 85.
9. *The Catholic Mind* 38 (8 January 1940): 1–9.
10. *The New York Times*, 25 December 1939, 1.

with the exception of the bloodstained lands of Poland and Finland—the number of victims [of the war] can be considered lower than it was feared." It is difficult not to see Germany and the Soviets as the Pope's chief targets in this address, as the Western Allies had not yet launched any offensive action, and certainly neither was involved in Poland nor Finland.

Pius' Easter homily, March 24, 1940, said, "Pacts solemnly confirmed by agreement on both sides are continually being revised, or violated outright, at the discretion of one party, without any attempt at discussion and clear adjustment, of mutual relations"; "The laws which bind civilized people together have been violated; most lamentably undefended cities, country towns and villages, have been terrorized by bombing."[11] At this time, neither side had started heavy bombing of the other; but the Germans had bombed undefended Warsaw and other Polish cities during the invasion that began the war; the Soviets had done little bombing in their invasion of Poland. The only pacts that had been violated by that time were the German-Polish non-aggression pact of 1934, which the Germans broke by their invasion, and a similar pact between Poland and the Soviets.

On May 10, 1940, following the German invasion of the West, Pius sent a telegram to each of the rulers of Belgium, the Netherlands, and Luxembourg.[12] In these, he commiserated with them and called the invasion "against right," and "against all justice." These telegrams were made public in *L'Osservatore Romano*, which went on to write that "the total war launched by Germany has clearly revealed itself as a pitiless war of extermination conducted in defiance of the laws of war."[13]

There were two public addresses concerning the fall of France

11. Charles Rankin, *The Pope Speaks* (New York: Harcourt Brace, 1940) 248ff.

12. *ADSS* 1:413–14.

13. *L'Osservatore Romano*, 12 May 1940, 1, 13–14.

in the summer of 1940. The first was a response to the presentation of credentials of Wladimir d'Ormesson, the new French Ambassador on June 9, 1940, shortly before the armistice; the second was a "Letter to the French Church" after the establishment of the Vichy regime. In both addresses Pius extended sympathy to the French nation, but did not condemn an aggressor.[14]

On November 24, 1940, the Pope delivered "An Appeal to the World for a Just Peace."[15] He said that he "had done everything for peace among nations," and he offered a prayer for the victims of the war. He asked God to "give to the combatants . . . that noble sense of humanity by which they will not, no matter in what circumstances, do to others that which they would not have done to themselves or to their country." He concluded by asking for "a new and harmonious prosperity, true and well-ordered peace that will permanently unite as brothers, through the ages, all peoples of the human race."

His second Christmas message of the war was delivered on December 24, 1940.[16] Again, he lamented the fact that the "laws and morality of international warfare have been so callously ignored." He talked about the help and hope the Holy See was giving the prisoners of war, and he mentioned all the countries involved; further, that "We have been able, by the help of Our representatives and by Our own subsidy, to give support to a great number of refugees, homeless and emigrants—including also non-aryans."

He predicted that a new world order would arise out of the war, that there could be no return to the pre-war settlement, and said that "in the strife of opinions, the Church cannot be invoked to listen to one side more than to another." Did this mean that the German "New Order" was as acceptable as the British

14. *The Tablet*, 31 July 1940, 150. Rankin, 259–61.
15. *The Catholic Mind* 38 (22 December 1940): 521–529.
16. *The Catholic Mind* 39 (8 January 1941): 1–8.

aims for a civilized Europe? He went on to posit the premises for such a new order, that it would be based on the "natural ideals of Truth, Justice, and Charity," opposed to the idea that "might can create right," and by "a genuine Christian solidarity of a legal and economic character." It is difficult to see how the German "New Order" could meet these premises.

His first major address in 1941 was his Easter message of April 13.[17] This was another plea for peace. At this time, the German army, with its Hungarian, Romanian, and Bulgarian allies had just invaded Yugoslavia and was on its way toward Greece. The Italians had invaded Greece in the fall of 1940 and had been pushed back into Albania, but they now joined in the invasion of Greece. The British had sent forces to help the Greeks. It was also a period of the continuing blitz of England by German bombers, and a corresponding but lesser bombing of Germany by English bombers.

In this address, the Pope acknowledged the fact that many were fighting out of a deep sense of loyalty to their fatherlands, but that "the ruthless struggle has at times assumed forms that can only be described as atrocious." He remarked that there appeared "as yet little likelihood of an approximate realization of peace that will be just." As for the treatment of civilians, "Remember that upon the manner in which you deal with those whom the fortunes of war put in your hands may depend the blessing or curse of God on your own fatherland." This stricture can apply to Germany, Italy, and the Soviets, which were the only occupying powers at the time, although the British held large numbers of Italians prisoners of war in Africa.

On June 29, 1941, shortly after the German invasion of the Soviet Union, Pius delivered an address on the occasion of the feast of Saints Peter and Paul.[18] In it he lamented the sufferings

17. *The Catholic Mind* 39 (22 April 1941): 1–8.
18. *The Catholic Mind* 39 (8 August 1941): 1–10.

of people caught up in the war, military as well as civilian, and referred specifically to blockades causing famine. The British were blockading the Continent at that time, and while there were serious shortages of food in some countries as a result, the effect of the blockade on the French was moderated by the secret agreement the British had with Vichy France to allow some shipments through from the United States. The one area that was greatly affected by the blockade was Greece, but not until later in that year. But the main purpose of the address was to answer the question of how God could permit such a tragedy, especially to the innocent who were caught up with the guilty in the war. Pius had no answer except to point out that God can draw good out of evil, and that suffering is the common lot of mankind.

His Christmas message of December 24, 1941,[19] found Germany at war with the Soviets, and the United States at war, allied with the Soviets and Britain against the Axis powers. The Germans had just been turned away from the gates of Moscow but remained deep inside Russia. Already large numbers of Jews were being killed in German-occupied Russia and Poland, and some deportations had already begun.

The message had all of the traditional sorrow that the earlier Christmas messages had: sorrow for the people suffering as a result of the war (in all of these messages, there is a concern for the vast debts caused by the war and the economic havoc that would result). He addressed the question of why Christianity had failed and answered that people had perverted Christianity: true Christianity had not failed. The duty of the more powerful states, he said, was to respect the rights of the smaller states; under a new moral order, "there is no place for open or occult oppression of the cultural and linguistic characteristics of national minorities," and the governments must respect the rights of minorities. "We love," he continued, "with equal affection all peo-

19. *The Catholic Mind* 40 (8 January 1942): 1–20.

ples, without any exception whatsoever, and in order to avoid even the appearance of being moved by partisanship, we have maintained hitherto the greatest reserve."

On May 13, 1942, on the occasion of Pius' silver jubilee of his consecration as a bishop, he addressed "Pleas to the Warring Nations."[20] The Church, he said, was under attack "in some countries" and he talked of "combative atheism, systematic anti-Christianity" and the sufferings of clergy "in some places." He made a fresh appeal for peace "now when the nations are living in the painful suspense of waiting for new engagements to begin," and he assured them of "Our absolute impartiality towards all the belligerents and with equal affection for all peoples without exception." Did Pius, who was always very careful with his words, make clear that his affection was for peoples, not governments? At the time, the German armies were deep in Russia, advancing in the Caucasus; they had pushed the British back in North Africa. The United States was on the defensive in the Pacific. This was the height of Axis power.

His Christmas message of December 24, 1942, came at a time when the tide was turning.[21] The Anglo-American forces had invaded North Africa and were on the offensive against the Germans. The Battle of Stalingrad was in its final days. By this time, the Pope certainly knew something of the wholesale massacre of the Jews. The Church, he said, "does not intend to take sides for any of the particular forms in which the several peoples and States strive to solve the gigantic problems of domestic order or international collaboration, as long as these forms conform to the Law of God." Pius knew the suffering of all peoples "without exception" and he wanted to bring them any help he could.

Then, in one of the most-frequently cited phrases by his defenders, he said that all of the "magnanimous and upright"

20. *The Catholic Mind* 40 (8 June 1942): 1–19.
21. *The Catholic Mind* 40 (January 1943): 45–60.

should make a solemn vow to reestablish a just society: "Mankind owes that vow" to the dead in battle, to the civilians who have been hurt by the war, and "mankind owes that vow to the hundreds of thousands of persons who, without any fault on their part, sometimes only because of their nationality or race, have been consigned to death or to a slow decline." When the American chargé, Harold Tittmann asked the Pope about this message, Pius said he thought that he had made it "plain to everyone that he was referring to the Poles, Jews and hostages." Furthermore, Pius said that, "when talking of atrocities he could not name the Nazis without at the same time mentioning the Bolsheviks and this, he thought, might not be wholly pleasing to the Allies."[22] The German Ambassador to the Holy See was told by Ribbentrop, the German Foreign Minister, to protest this Christmas message because the Pope, he said, was deserting his neutrality,[23] and the RSHA (Nazi Security Office) report on the speech accused Pius of making himself "the mouthpiece of the Jewish war criminals."[24]

When he made his patronal address on June 2, 1943,[25] the Allied armies were on the verge of total control of North Africa. At the Casablanca Conference in January the Allied leaders had enunciated the doctrine of unconditional surrender. Italy was being threatened with invasion.

The occasion for the address was the Pope's feast day of St. Eugene. He said his words had been twisted. "We lend Our ear with particularly profound sympathy to the voice of those who turn to Us imploringly." Then, he made another of his frequently cited phrases:

22. Harrison to Hull, 5 January 1943, *FRUS* 1943: 2:911–12.

23. As cited in Chadwick, *Britain and the Vatican*, 218–19.

24. As cited in Anthony Rhodes, *The Vatican in the Age of the Dictators (1922–1945)* (New York: Holt, Rinehart and Winston, 1973), 272–73.

25. *The Catholic Mind* 41 (September 1943): 1–5.

They are those who, because of their nationality or descent, are pursued by mounting misfortune and increasing suffering. Sometimes, through no fault of theirs, they are subjected to measures which threaten them with extermination. . . . Every single word in Our statements addressed to the competent authorities, and every one of Our public utterances, has had to be weighed and pondered by Us with deep gravity, in the very interest of those who are suffering, so as not to render their position even more difficult and unbearable than before, be it unwittingly and unintentionally. . . . We do not forget a single one of the suffering peoples . . . even if at the present moment We wish to direct your compassion in a special manner to the Polish people.

Three million Polish Jews were either already dead or threatened with death by that time. Did Pius include them in his compassion? They were, after all, part of the Polish people.

By the time of his Christmas message, December 24, 1943, Italy had surrendered, Rome and most of Italy were under German control, and in October Jews had been rounded up in Rome. The Soviets were pushing the Germans back. Greeks were starving to death. In the Balkans, the Ustashe had proclaimed a Catholic state and were killing Orthodox Serbs. In the message,[26] Pius railed against those "who placed all their faith in a world expansion of economic life," and those who put their faith in "Godless science," not "true science." The war was a disaster, he said, and asking what could be done, he responded, "We have used and shall use all Our resources, material and spiritual, to lessen the sad consequences of the war for prisoners, wounded, missing, starving, needy—for all those in suffering and in trouble of every language and nation." Those who had ignored Christian teaching are responsible for the "disaster which today overwhelms the world."

When he made his patronal address on June 2, 1944,[27] Rome was on the verge of being liberated by the Allies. He pleaded

26. *The Catholic Mind* 42 (February 1944): 65–76.
27. *The Catholic Mind* 42 (July 1944): 386–93.

against the destruction of Rome, calling it "matricide." He protested against those who wanted a "complete victory," undoubtedly an allusion to the Allied doctrine of unconditional surrender, and talked about the threat such a tactic posed to a stable
peace.

Through the summer of 1944 (Rome had been liberated on
June 6), Pius gave a number of addresses to different groups of
Allied soldiers, many of which were published; there is no
record of any of the addresses given to German soldiers during
the years that Italy was a member of the Axis, although he held
general audiences for everyone during those years. According to
Pius' secretary, Robert Lieber, once the German occupation of
Rome began, German authorities forbade German soldiers to attend papal audiences.[28]

When he gave his address on the fifth anniversary of the outbreak of the war on September 1, 1944,[29] it should have been
apparent to everyone that Germany was on the verge of defeat.
The Allies had liberated France and were poised for the drive
into Germany. But there were still battles in northern Italy. The
Soviets were in Poland, but not yet at Warsaw. The attempted assassination of Hitler had taken place. Through all of the papal
rhetoric, Pius urged collaboration with former enemies (a refer-
ence to Allies working with Germans, or perhaps to Italians to
come together?). Much of this address was concerned with the
continuing war in the north of Italy and the needs of civilians
in wartime. He talked about the future and the need for a peace
based on Christian principles. He again defended the right of
private property (against the Communists?) and supported the
proposal for the United Nations.

Throughout the fall of 1944, he addressed various groups, in-

28. "Pius as I Knew Him," *The Catholic Mind* 57 (1959): 301 (trans. Roland
Hill in *The Tablet*, 13, 20, 27 December 1958, from *Stimmen der Zeit*, November 1958).

29. *The Catholic Mind* 42 (October 1944): 577–86.

cluding Poles and some members of the United States Congress.

When he issued his Christmas message on December 24, 1944,[30] the end of the war was in sight. Soviet armies had over-run Poland. There was still fighting in northern Italy. Allied armies were bogged down in Belgium, but obviously the Germans could not hold out much longer. Many details of the German death camps were becoming known. The message chiefly warned of the problems of peace, the fallacies of democracy, and the need to distinguish between true and false democracy. It addressed the matter of punishment for war crimes: he urged that individuals, not whole communities be punished. He also thanked various countries for helping fund aid for the Holy See to distribute.

The last of his public statements on the war was his patronal address of June 2, 1945,[31] which followed the surrender of Germany the previous month. In this address he justified his policy toward Germany's Third Reich. He said he had foreseen the disaster of the war, which had followed "the ideas and activities of a State which took no heed of the most sacred ideals of mankind." He spoke of the negotiations for the concordat in 1933, that "since it was the German Government that made the proposal, the responsibility for all regrettable consequences would have fallen on the Holy See if the proposed Concordat had been declined." Furthermore, the agreement did not mean any formal approval of Nazism, and "it must be recognized that the Concordat in the years that followed brought some advantages, or at least prevented worse evils." Nonetheless, the Nazi state had continued to persecute the Church: Catholic schools, press, and organizations had been suppressed and religious houses confiscated: "To resist such attacks, millions of coura-

---

30. *The Catholic Mind* 43 (February 1945): 65–67.
31. *The Tablet*, 9 June 1945, 268–70.

geous Catholic men and women closed their ranks around their Bishops, whose valiant and severe pronouncements never failed to resound, even in these last years of the war."

He talked of Pius XI's encyclical *Mit Brennender Sorge*, which condemned the doctrines of Nazism, and said, "No one can accuse the Church of not having denounced and exposed in time the true nature of the National-Socialist movement and the danger to which it exposed Christian civilization." And, the Pope said, he himself had, especially in his broadcast addresses, "constantly opposed the demands and the perennial laws of humanity and of the Christian Faith to the ruinous and inexorable application of National-Socialist teachings, which even went so far as to use the most exquisite scientific methods to torture or eliminate people who were often innocent."

He praised the many clergy and "numberless Catholics" who had been imprisoned and killed by the Nazis for "their fidelity to Christ." He cited the statistics from the concentration camp of Dachau: 2800 Polish clergy imprisoned, only 816 left alive at the end of the war, and 840 German clergy, including 45 Protestant ministers, imprisoned in Dachau, along with numerous priests imprisoned and killed at other sites under German control.

As for the future, he hoped that Germany "can rise to a new dignity and a new life, when once it has cast off the Satanic specter raised by National-Socialism, and when the guilty, as We have already at other times had occasion to expound, have expiated the crimes they have committed." This was his last public comment on the war.

Finally, there is the question of the broadcasts from Radio Vatican and the articles in *L'Osservatore Romano*. Did Pius approve the exact wording of each one? If he did not, the fact remains that those who broadcast and those who published were allowed to do so at the sufferance of Pius, and presumably he would not have allowed them to say and write the things they did if he had disapproved. Both of these media present a curious problem, for both were clearly pro-Allied during the first part of the war. Since there was never any question in the minds of any of the warring powers that both spoke for the Pope, their statements compromised his stated neutrality, and he must have known it.

Vatican Radio was largely under control of the Jesuit General Wladimir Ledochowski, a Pole. It broadcast news of German atrocities against priests and laymen in Poland in the first months of the war. A specific directive by the Pope was given in early 1940 for the radio to describe the condition of the Church in Poland.[32] Thus, on January 21, 1940, Vatican Radio said:

The Polish people, especially in those areas occupied by Germany, have been thrown into a state of terror, of degradation, and, we dare say, of barbarism, much akin to what the communists imposed on Spain in 1936. . . . The Germans employ the same methods, perhaps even worse, than those used by the Soviets. Even more violent and persistent has been the assault upon elementary justice and decency in that part of prostrate Poland which has fallen to German administration.[33]

Cardinal Hlond made a broadcast that angered the Germans; indeed throughout the first years of the war, the German government protested the pro-Allied bias of Vatican Radio. In response, Pius ordered that all broadcast texts be submitted in advance to the Vatican Secretary of State. The Germans continued to protest the broadcasts as anti-German. The radio programs appear innocuous in the reading but, seen in context, they criticized the Germans—to such an extent that in April 1941 the Germans and Italians demanded the end of such transmissions, and Pius gave in and ordered that Vatican Radio not mention Germany in the future.[34]

32. According to a note by Montini, 19 January 1940, *ADSS* 3:204–05.
33. As cited in Blet, *Pie XII*, 89–90.
34. Chadwick, *Britain and the Vatican*, 141–49; and Robert A. Graham, "La Radio Vaticana tra Londra e Berlino," *La Civiltà Cattolica* 3014 (17 January

L'Osservatore Romano, the Vatican daily, published the Pope's messages and statements. It also commented on the war news until May 1940, when, under pressure from the Italian government, it was forced to limit itself simply to reporting the news without comment. But it was considered pro-Allied by the Axis powers. It occasionally printed the texts of Vatican Radio broadcasts that the Germans and Italians had protested. And there were issues that openly protested the persecution of Jews: surprisingly, after Mussolini had been ousted from power by the King, and then restored to a puppet status under the German occupation, *L'Osservatore* protested against the government's order to collect the Jews for transportation to concentration camps. The paper called the order "unreasonable, unchristian, and inhuman."[35] It is difficult to deny that this newspaper had the full support of the Pope, who, after all, was the sovereign of the Vatican state and by law the publisher of *L'Osservatore Romano*.

Pius' Private Views

Did Pius' private views correspond to his public expressions? These private views can be found in the diplomatic correspondence. The Pope talked regularly with the diplomats accredited to the Holy See. He was, of course, most anxious to prevent the spread of the war, and he wanted to use his diplomatic skills to do so. Thus, his diplomatic language was, on the one hand, less direct and more conciliatory where he found it necessary—chiefly in dealing with the German diplomats—and on the other hand, more direct and less conciliatory when dealing with the Allied representatives. While critics argue that this indicates Pius' preference for Germany's cause, it seems more likely, in view of

---

1976): 132–50. Blet, *Pie XII*, 114–21, has a detailed discussion of Vatican Radio.

35. 3 December 1943, 1.

his other statements, that the reason for this two-sided approach was that he feared the Germans would continue the persecution of the Poles and other innocent people, and his words of conciliation might have an effect to moderate them, whereas he did not fear the Allies and found them more amenable to strong statements condemning bombing of civilians. The Allies did not persecute innocent people as a primary aim; the worst that can be said of them is that they terror-bombed in order to bring the war to an end. The Germans wanted a racially pure *Grossraum* and were determined to kill, enslave, or otherwise persecute noncombatants to accomplish their end. This appears to explain the sometimes contradictory private conversations of the Pope.

One example is his moderating the complaints in his encyclical *Summi Pontificatus* to Fritz Menshausen, the German chargé at the Vatican. According to Menshausen, Pius assured him that he was not opposed to totalitarian states, that he was waiting for reciprocation from Germany for readiness to "reach an understanding" and, that to charges that the Allies were interpreting the papal pronouncements as being directed against Germany, the Pope said the "pronouncements were naturally only general in character and that, over and above this, he was always particularly concerned to phrase them in such a manner that they could not be misunderstood by Germany as being directed against that country."[36]

How could the Pope say that he was not opposed to totalitarian states when he had condemned the deification of the state and totalitarian aims in his October encyclical? Was Pius playing a double diplomatic game, saying one thing to the public at large and another to Germans in private? Or was Menshausen telling his superiors what they wanted to hear rather than the truth?

36. Friedlander, *Pius XII*, 40–41, citing telegram from Menshausen to Berlin, 1 January 1940.

Pius was never sure what the Germans would do; he had a better idea of how the Allies would respond to his words. Thus, he could criticize the Allied bombing of Rome to Osborne, the British Minister to the Holy See, and get responses from the British government, whereas his complaints about German treatment of the Polish people were met with silence from Berlin.[37]

Another example of this inconsistency is his meeting with Joachim von Ribbentrop, the German Foreign Minister, in March 1940, six months after the invasion and conquest of Poland. In response to Ribbentrop's complaints about Pius' Christmas message, in which the Pope had criticized "premeditated aggressions against a small laborious and peaceful people on the pretext of a threat which neither exists, nor is desired, nor is possible," Pius told the German Foreign Minister that the "small laborious and peaceful people" of his Christmas message was the Finns.[38]

What about the nuncios and the papal Secretary of State? When a nuncio spoke, was he speaking at the direction of the Pope, or was he using his own reading of the situation? Luigi Maglione, the Secretary of State, sympathized with Allied diplomats at the Vatican, and in September 1942, he answered their complaints that the Pope had not made a strong enough protest against German treatment of the Jews and other oppressed people by telling them that Pius would soon clarify his protests.[39] Did he clear this and other statements with the Pope, or did he have discretionary powers? On the surface it would appear that Pius, by training, was a careful enough diplomat not to let anyone say anything about which he did not approve, at least in theory if not in substance. His nuncios confirmed this.[40] On the

37. Chadwick, *Rome and the Vatican*, 227, 285; Falconi, *Silence*, 134.

38. *ADSS* 1:356. Tardini's notes of the conversation, told to him by Pius, 11 March 1940.

39. *ADSS* 5:721.

40. Rhodes, *Vatican*, 340.

other hand, Chadwick says that Maglione and Pius were often at odds over issues, and that the Secretary of State frequently did what he wanted and then Pius went along with him.[41] Yet doubts still remain, and the critics and defenders of the Pope pick and choose among all these various statements to prove their points.

Papal Rhetoric

Popes have seldom spoken in direct simple sentences. Pius, the trained diplomat, was even less direct than most. Reading encyclicals and other papal statements often requires interpretive skills to determine just exactly what is said. As a result, people can read into some papal words what they want to hear. And looked at in hindsight, Pius' words of protest fall short when measured against the horror of the Nazi machinery of destruction. We ask today how the Pope's words could have had any effect at all.

However, it is argued that this was not the case in wartime Europe. Beate Ruhm von Oppen says that "to someone unversed in the codeword dialectics of the period" the Pope's words "often sound like collaboration;" but to the German regime, they "register resistance." One must understand "the differing linguistic usage of the times;" and while "this may sound like hairsplitting . . . it was by such split hairs that friend and foe recognized each other while the conflict was on."[42]

Historian Vesna Drapac is even more explicit. In her study of the Church in occupied Paris during the war, she says, "The language that is peculiar to the Church must be understood if its pronouncements are to be appreciated fully. It constitutes a sort of code and one must have the key to that code. . . . Under au-

---

41. Chadwick, *Britain and the Vatican,* 53–54.
42. "Nazis and Christians," 393, 410.

thoritarian regimes language becomes complicated. . . . Meanings were 'hidden' or 'ambiguous' only to those unfamiliar with the language's devices."[43]

Jesuit Robert A. Graham, one of the Pope's most vigorous defenders, concurs: "It is true that the papal language, in these circumstances, was indirect, round-about and imprecise. But there was no doubt, for those who care to read, as to what he meant."[44]

What the Germans Thought of Pius' Public Statements

There appears to be little question that throughout the war the German government believed that Pius was criticizing them and that he was on the side of the Allies. Pius cannot have been unaware of this belief, and, given his desire to mediate the conflict, this may in fact have been the chief reason why he constantly stated his neutrality, saying that his concern extended to all peoples.

Hitler had no regard for the Pope nor indeed for the Church. In his nightly ramblings, he said that he intended to abrogate the concordat once the war was over and to end the state's subsidy to the Church; further, he would exact retribution from clergy who had opposed him or Nazism in any way.[45] He ignored the Vatican's complaints about violations of the concordat. The officials in the German government followed this policy as well.

The Nazi regime's general policy toward any papal or Vatican protests and criticisms was to remain silent, to refuse to answer,

43. *War and Religion: Catholics in the Churches of Occupied Paris* (Washington: The Catholic University of America Press, 1998), 23–24.

44. "How to Manufacture a Legend," in *Pius XII and the Holocaust* (Milwaukee: Catholic League for Religious and Civil Rights, 1988), 21.

45. *Hitler's Secret Conversations, 1941–1944,* trans. N. Cameron and R. Stevens (New York: Farrar, Strauss, and Cudahy, 1953), 516–20.

and to ignore the nuncio, Cesare Orsenigo. It held to this policy with few exceptions.[46] Government officials believed that most Catholics were solidly behind the nation's war effort and that few Catholics read papal statements in any event. The German bishops, with very few exceptions, supported the war as well; their response to papal criticism of the regime was that the Pope was criticizing the government for its attacks upon the Church and for violations of the concordat, not the German war machine or the persecution of occupied peoples. But once the war began, Hitler decided that nothing should be done to exacerbate relations with the Vatican. The German war effort depended upon the support of all Germans, and he did not want to do anything to alienate Catholic support.

46. See Conway, *The Nazi Persecution of the Churches*, 239ff.

Chapter 5

An Examination of the Reasons
The Least Likely

On the surface, it would seem to be a simple matter to determine the reasons why Pope Pius did not issue a strong statement denouncing the German treatment of defenseless civilians, including the destruction of the Jews. Through the verbiage of papal rhetoric, one can clearly discern Pius' fear that such a statement would expose the Jews and other victims of Nazi terror to worse harm. He confirmed this explicitly in private to confidantes. But one can detect inconsistencies in his statements, and he did not say things that critics say he should have said. Undoubtedly Pius had other reasons for not sending a strong statement.

It is the inconsistencies in Pius' statements, both public and private, and in his actions that provide the basis for the controversy regarding his alleged silence. Most defenders and critics start with a particular point of view and use the documentary evidence to bolster their contentions. Few observers—historians or journalists—start from a disinterested position and allow the documents to determine their conclusions.

Added to this problem is the difficulty of proving a negative. It is easier to determine why the Pope did something than it is to find out why he did *not* do something. Such a concern raises all sorts of logical problems.

In examining the reasons that historians and journalists offer for the Pope's alleged silence, from what appears to be the least likely reason to the most likely, it is important to keep in mind that it is probable that Pius acted from more than one motive.

Pius as an Anti-Semite

There is, of course, a long tradition of anti-Semitism in all of the Christian churches. Modern historians, since the Holocaust, distinguish between anti-Semitism, which is based on a racial criterion, and anti-Judaism, which is based on religion. The Nazis did not accept a Jew who had converted to Christianity as a Christian: racially that person was still a Jew.

While this distinction was not made in all periods of church history, certainly by the twentieth century most Catholic churchmen accepted a converted Jew as a Catholic in the full sense of the word. They made no distinction based on the race or ethnicity of any Catholic. The Nuremberg Laws, however, did: a Jew was a Jew, no matter what his or her religion.

There is little question that the Holocaust had its origin in the centuries-long hostility felt by Christians against Jews. There were pogroms in the Middle Ages. Jews faced legal and religious restrictions right up to the twentieth century in many countries. The popes, when they were monarchs of the Papal States, established ghettoes in the cities they controlled and forced the Jews to attend periodic sermons, along with other restrictions. But, as clearly demonstrated in the notorious nineteenth-century Mortara Affair in which a Jewish child, secretly baptized by a Catholic domestic servant, was forcibly taken from his parents and raised by Pope Pius IX as a Catholic, once baptized, a Jew was a Christian, without any regard to his previous religious beliefs.[1]

Many Central European Christians were anti-Semites; so were many Western Europeans, as the Dreyfus Affair clearly demonstrates. The responsibility of the Catholic Church in inculcating and fostering this attitude is beyond dispute. What is a matter of concern here is whether or not Pius' behavior was the result of this residual anti-Semitism.

Was Pius himself an anti-Semite? This is the unstated undercurrent in the arguments of many of Pius' strongest critics. Few say it outright, because they regard it as a fact—taken for granted—given the history of the papacy and Pius' background in the hothouse of ecclesiastical politics and training in the late nineteenth and early twentieth centuries, where Jews were viewed not only as "Christ-killers" but more importantly as purveyors of a cultural modernism at variance with traditional Christianity. It is also the simplest explanation for critics of the Pope. It requires no extensive examination of the documents or memoirs; indeed it requires none at all, for the fact is made obvious. The Pope was the leader of an organization that had been anti-Semitic for centuries, that had condoned the persecution of Jews in all countries, even as late as the nineteenth century. Why would one expect the Pope to have reacted otherwise to the Nazi persecution of the Jews?

In his examination of the literature on the subject, Giovanni Miccoli finds this attitude to be widely prevalent. He says, "The tradition of Catholic anti-Semitism, which obviously is not to be confounded with Nazi racism, is indicated [by many] as an explanation not only of the silence of Pius XII but also of the ex-

1. David Kertzer, *The Kidnapping of Edgardo Mortara* (New York: Knopf, 1997).

istence of systems of thought and of a comprehensive culture which rendered the Holocaust possible."[2] Perhaps the most extreme statement of this position is taken by the American religious historian Richard L. Rubenstein who says that "over time I have become convinced that during World War II Pope Pius XII and the vast majority of European Christian leaders regarded the elimination of the Jews as no less beneficial than the destruction of Bolshevism."[3] Continuing this amazing interpretation, he compares Pius to Pope Innocent III in his struggle against the Albigensians in the thirteenth century, and says that both popes were confronted with "dangerous external and internal threats" and that while Innocent prescribed the sword against the Albigensians, Pius was no less guilty in his attitude toward the Jews, whom he perceived as a threat to Western Christendom. Rubenstein cites no primary sources for this astounding explanation of Pius' behavior.

The English journalist John Cornwell, argues that Pius was anti-Semitic, using as proof an account of a meeting of Pacelli's aide, Lorenzo Schioppa, with the Bavarian Soviet in 1919, when Pacelli was nuncio to Bavaria. It is not known whether Schioppa told Pacelli, who then wrote a memorandum to the Vatican Secretary of State in Rome, or Schioppa wrote the memorandum himself and then Pacelli edited it and signed it. The memorandum identifies the head of the Soviet "rabble" as a Jew and mentions "a gang of young women of dubious appearance, Jews like all the rest of them, hanging around in all the offices with lecherous demeanor and suggestive smiles."[4] In response, Pierre Blet argues that the letter had probably been written by

2. Giovanni Miccoli, "Aspetti e problemi del pontificato de Pio XII," 343.

3. "A Twentieth-Century Journey," in *From the Unthinkable to the Unavoidable*, ed. Carol Rittner and John K. Roth (Westport, Conn.: Greenwood, 1997), 167.

4. *Hitler's Pope*, 74–75. The document is in Fattorini, 322–25.

Schioppa and "its derogatory references were not religious in nature but political."[5] Historian Istvan Deak, not sympathetic to Pius in general, finds the comment "[not] convincing . . . proof of Pacelli's anti-Semitism."[6]

The popular writer Gitta Sereny is also convinced that the Pope's anti-Semitism was a factor in his behavior. She says, "Anyone who has read Pius XII's letters to the German bishops . . . must find it difficult to doubt that the Pope was anti-Semitic."[7] A moderate position is taken by Meir Michaelis in his exhaustive study of the Italian Jews. He says that "while it is true that the Vatican did not consider 'defensive' measures against Jews in conflict with Catholic teaching, it is equally true that Pius XII was profoundly shocked at Hitler's method of solving the Jewish problem."[8] John T. Pawlikowski, a priest, has been one of the more able critics of the problem of Pius and the Holocaust. He contends that "we are on safe scholarly grounds in asserting that traditional Christian anti-Semitism was not a principal determinant of the Vatican's approach."[9] Supporting this assertion is the statement of Adriano Ossicini, who said that Pius refused to meet with the Italian royal family in January 1940 if Mussolini was to be present. Ossicini claims Pius said, "I don't want anyone present at the meeting who signed the racial laws [of 1938]".[10] Although critical of Pius for other reasons, Michael Marrus offers the most widely used defense against the

5. Cited in John Thavis, "Vatican Expert's Book Defends WWII Policies of Pope Pius XII," 11 October 1999. <http://www.catholic.org/media/news>

6. "The Pope, the Nazis and the Jews," *New York Review of Books*, 23 March 2000, 46.

7. *Into That Darkness* (New York: McGraw Hill, 1974), 283.

8. *Mussolini and the Jews* (Oxford: Clarendon Press, 1978), 374.

9. "The Vatican and the Holocaust," 307.

10. Reported in *Avvenire* (Rome), 27 June 1996, from cwnews.com., but here again this is unsubstantiated hearsay.

argument of the Pope's alleged anti-Semitism. He points out that the Pope did not vociferously protest German treatment of the Poles, who were an eminently Catholic people.[11] This negative argument is also made by Richard Lukas in his study, *The Forgotten Holocaust: The Poles under German Occupation 1939–1944*.[12] Thus, if the critics' argument is unstated but implicit, so also Pius' defenders' argument is similarly unstated but implicit. They argue that Pius' public protests were general, not specific. He publicly sympathized with the oppressed peoples, but did not take the extra step of condemning their oppressors by name. If he did not do for the Catholic Poles what he did not do for the Jews, then, they argue, it would be difficult to label Pius as an anti-Semite. However, this contention shows the difficulty of proving a negative, for logically, Pius could have been anti-Polish as well, a thought that occurred to some Poles, as will be seen. Further, Susan Zuccotti says that indeed, a protest against the persecution of the Poles would have made things worse for them, but a protest in favor of the Jews would have "warned other Jews to hide and convinced more Christians to open their doors to them."[13]

Many critics also contend that Pius was interested only in the plight of Jews who had converted to Catholicism. As proof, they cite the attempts of the Vatican to obtain visas for these converted Jews to escape Europe to Brazil. One attempt came at the request of Bishop Berning of Osnabrück to bring about the emigration of converted German Jews. After many problems were encountered and after some of these converts were allowed to emigrate, the project was eventually dropped because of opposition by the Brazilian government.[14] Attempts were made to obtain the same concessions for converted Jews in other countries.

11. *The Holocaust in History*, 179–83.
12. Lexington: University Press of Kentucky, 1986, ix.
13. Zuccotti, 97
14. Morley, 18–21.

Thus, the critics charge, Pius was interested only in converted Jews and did not make the same attempts for other Jews.

John Conway responds to this argument by pointing out that converted Jews were Catholics and therefore could legally claim Church intervention in countries where a concordat governed relations. More importantly, converted Jews were considered renegades by Jews and therefore were without support in the Jewish communities. Their plight was immediately demanding. Finally, as Catholics, an appeal was possible to such Catholic countries as Brazil and Spain to take them in.[15]

Pius Was Concerned about the Security of the Vatican

In her study of the Vatican and the Holocaust in Italy, Susan Zuccotti contends that the primary explanation for the lack of a papal protest was that "above all else, Pius XII feared for the integrity of the Vatican itself."[16] If Mussolini's Fascists or the Germans invaded the Vatican, then the functioning of the Church would be severely handicapped. In effect, the government of the Church would be impaired, and all of the administrative functions so necessary to the meeting of its international obligations would be so damaged that it might never recover. For the Pope, who was after all the chief administrator of the Church, this was a serious concern.

Relations between the Holy See and the Italian State were governed by the Lateran Accords, signed in 1929 to settle the decades-long Roman Question. According to the Treaty, Italy recognized the Vatican as a sovereign state with full rights of access for diplomats and church officials, with a guaranteed supply of water, connection to telephone, telegraph, and radio services, and freedom of trade. The agreement also regulated relations

15. "The Vatican, Germany and the Holocaust," 110–11.
16. Zuccotti, 315.

between Italy and the Holy See. In the event that Italy went to war, Article 24 of the Treaty stated that the Holy See "declares that it wishes to remain and will remain extraneous to all temporal disputes between States and to international congresses held for such objects, unless the contending parties make concordant appeal to its peaceful mission; at the same time reserving the right to exercise its moral and spiritual power."[17]

This article was ambiguous at best. If one of the contending parties in a war was violating moral standards, did the Pope have the right to condemn it without at the same time compromising his neutrality? What if the contending party was Italy? Presumably the Lateran Treaty was written on the basis of the experience of World War I, in which there were few war crimes; but none of the belligerents in that war was governed by a pagan ideology, as Nazism was in World War II.

Did the Lateran Treaty restrict the Pope? Was he afraid that by condemning one side, he would be accused of partisanship; and that by doing so he would be violating the Treaty, which could then be abrogated by Italy? Such an action would put intolerable pressure on the Pope, as the Vatican, being entirely within Italian territory, could be denied even the basic necessities of water and food. There is no doubt that Pius was concerned, and it must have been one of the reasons for his unsuccessful attempts to prevent Italy from joining Germany in the war. He was also concerned to not antagonize Mussolini. During the interregnum between Pius XI's death and his election, he assured the Italian Ambassador to the Holy See that Pius XI's last undelivered address, a criticism of Fascism, would be put in the secret archives and not published; this was an attempt at conciliation with Mussolini's government.[18]

17. Cited in John Pollard, *The Vatican and Italian Fascism, 1929–32* (Cambridge: Cambridge University Press, 1985), 203.
18. Chadwick, *Britain and the Vatican*, 34.

In fact, as time went on, Pius must have realized that a Fascist invasion or threat to the Vatican would have been a serious blunder on Mussolini's part, given the popular image of the Pope among the Italian populace. It is difficult to believe that such a threat would have hindered him from speaking out. When the Germans occupied Rome in 1943, it was a different matter. Although the Germans respected the Lateran Treaty and did not violate it, there was always the fear that Hitler could decide at any moment to invade the Vatican, or to shut off services. Even given Hitler's desire to put his opposition to the Pope and the Church on hold until the end of the war, such a scenario remained a possibility and therefore a concern to the Pope and the Curia. But it hardly seems possible that this was a major reason for the alleged papal silence, especially since the German occupation of Rome came relatively late in the war and lasted only nine months.

The Pope's Personal Fear of Capture or Imprisonment

Did Pius fear that Hitler might seize the Vatican and kidnap him? However unlikely such an action might be, for Hitler was fearful of the reaction of German Catholics to such a move, Vatican officials had to be concerned. Albrecht von Kessel, German Ambassador Weizsäcker's counselor, claims that after the German occupation of Rome in September 1943, Hitler considered kidnapping the Pope, and "we had definite information that had the Pope resisted, he would have been shot while trying to escape."[19] On the other hand, Weizsäcker says in his memoirs that before he left to take up his assignment at the Vatican, Hitler

19. "The Pope and the Jews," in Bentley, ed., *Storm over the Deputy*, 75 (trans. from article in *Die Welt*, Hamburg, 6 April 1963).

agreed with his diplomatic policy of "mutual non-interven-tion."[20] One of the first critics of the Pope, Gerald Reitlinger, says that Pius' unwillingness to protest the deportation of Jews from Rome "proceeded neither from subtle benevolence nor from the Pope's possibly pro-German and positively anti-Soviet prejudices. It was, rather, the effect of plain physical fear."[21]

There were rumors earlier, when Italy entered the war, that Pius was prepared to go to neutral Spain or Portugal if the Ital-ian government threatened him; then, when the Germans occu-pied Rome, the rumor was spread by British propaganda opera-tives, that a castle had been prepared in Württemberg for a kidnapped Pope.[22] German Ambassador Weizsäcker says that he asked the German military authorities in Rome if such a plan ex-isted, and none could confirm it, but none could deny it either.[23] Both of these scenarios appear unlikely, especially that spread by the British. Of course, the Pope had to be concerned about the daily governance of the Church, as well as the humanitarian work the Holy See had undertaken, both of which would be halted by a German invasion of the Vatican and a possible kid-napping of the Pope. But he told Italian Ambassador Dino Alfieri that he had no fear of being sent to a concentration camp.[24] Carlo Falconi, one of Pius' most outspoken critics, does not believe Pius felt threatened. He says, "We can be very sure that Pius XII was not afraid. It would probably have been his finest hour if he could have provoked his own captivity by de-nouncing Nazi atrocities."[25]

20. *Memoirs of Ernst von Weizsäcker*, trans. John Andrews (Chicago: Hen-ry Regnery, 1951), 284.
21. *The Final Solution: The Attempt to Exterminate the Jews of Europe, 1939–1945*, 2d ed. (South Brunswick, N.J.: T. Yoseloff, 1968), 380.
22. Chadwick, *Britain and the Vatican*, 117–18, 275.
23. Weizsäcker, 291.
24. 13 May 1940, *ADSS* 1:422
25. *Silence*, 86–87.

Pius Feared the Destruction of Rome

If the three arguments—that Pius was an anti-Semite, that he was concerned about the security of the Vatican, and that he feared capture or imprisonment—do not appear to have been significant factors in his alleged silence, the question has been raised whether fear of the destruction of Rome might have been. There is little doubt that during the struggle for Italy and the occupation of Rome, the Pope was deeply concerned about preserving his beloved Rome from wartime destruction. Beginning in the summer of 1943, Allied planes bombed Roman railyards and arms depots; parts of the city were damaged, including churches and homes. There was violence in the streets during the German occupation, and some buildings were destroyed by fighting between the Germans and the Italian resistance groups, but the Germans generally avoided destructive action. The Germans also respected the extraterritoriality of designated religious buildings outside the Vatican, although Fascists loyal to Mussolini violated those buildings to seize anti-Fascists hiding in them.[26] As the Allies advanced from the south, Roman suburbs were shelled and the papal summer palace at Castelgandolfo was hit by Allied bombs. Pius implored D'Arcy Osborne, the British Minister to the Holy See, a number of times to beg the British government to spare Rome from aerial bombing.[27] The Pope also feared a possible German defensive destruction of the Eternal City when the Germans planned to evacuate Rome, but the German armies pulled out without incident. Ambassador Weiszäcker attributed the German protection of Rome to Hitler's "romantic feeling about the buildings of Rome."[28]

26. See Jane Scrivener (pseud.), *Inside Rome with the Germans* (New York: Macmillan, 1945). This diary of an American nun captures the violence and mood of tension during the nine months of occupation.

27. Chadwick, *Rome and the Vatican*, 240ff.

28. As cited in Chadwick, *Rome and the Vatican*, 288.

Historian Michael Phayer claims that Pius' fear of destruction of Rome was one of the two chief reasons for his unwillingness to speak out on the Holocaust. It was not just the treasures of the Eternal City that Pius wanted to protect; it was Rome as "the visible center of Catholicism." If Rome, the "nerve center of the Catholic faith," was destroyed, Phayer argues, then Pius feared that the Catholic states of Europe would be in peril. He blames Pius for putting the preservation of Rome ahead of the "moral issue of the murder of the Jews."[29] It could be argued that Phayer has overstated the case against Pius. He was, after all, the Bishop of Rome, and his concern certainly did register with both the Germans and the Allies, for the Germans avoided destruction and the Allied attacks were light compared to the bombing of other Axis cities. And although the Pope was concerned about Rome from the time Italy entered the war in June 1940, persecution of Jews was well underway by then; furthermore, the first bombing of Rome did not occur until the summer of 1943, more than a year after the Pope became aware of the systematic destruction of the Jews, and long after the alleged papal silence began. Given these circumstances, it would also appear that papal protests against the destruction of Rome cannot be viewed as an abandonment of the neutrality that Pius wanted to preserve to mediate the end of the war. Would a similar concern for the Jews have prompted the Germans to stop the Holocaust? This is a clear example of the cruel choice that Pius faced. He could be either the preserver of the institutional Church, or the Vicar of Christ: given the circumstances, he could not be both.

29. *Catholic Church*, 65.

Chapter 6

The Need for Protection
of German Catholics

The history of Pope Pius' relations with Hitler and his regime is clouded by controversy over the German bishops and their relations with the regime. This is a thorny issue that historians have sought to untangle, and their efforts at arriving at a consensus are little better than those concerning Pius and the Holocaust. The difficulty, for this analysis, is in working through the thicket of relations while keeping a focus on the Pope.

Let it be said at the outset that the German bishops, always with some exceptions, were scarred by Bismarck's Kulturkampf of the 1870s; they were particularly sensitive to the charge that they were not good Germans because they owed their allegiance to the Pope rather than to the German state. They felt this charge deeply, and as a result were inclined to give unqualified support to the nation, particularly in World War I.

When the war ended in 1918, the bishops feared the specter of Bolshevism, especially during and after the Spartacist uprising and in the subsequent Bavarian revolution in the Catholic heartland of Germany. Not a few identified the new Weimar regime with weakness in the face of this threat, and they furthermore saw it as a promoter of the general moral libertinism of the 1920s. When the Nazi movement began to gain support after 1930, most bishops recognized and condemned the pagan basis of Nazism, but they also saw Hitler as a forcible statesman who could revive Germany and restore not only its greatness, but also its moral values. They tended to discount his statist statements as election rhetoric, and they were pleased with his comments about the value of Christianity as the moral basis of the nation. Finally, once Hitler became Chancellor, most saw no other way out of the dilemma of the continued growth of Nazi power than to support the Vatican in its search for a concordat to regularize relations with the state.[1]

As a result of this episcopal predicament, the negotiation, observance, and importance of the German concordat of 1933 is one of the most misunderstood events in the history of Pope Pius XII's relations with Hitler's Reich. Beginning with Hochhuth's criticism, it has been argued that when he became pope, Pius should have abrogated the concordat, as a means of showing his disapproval of Hitler. But this argument rests on the notion that the concordat bestowed the Pope's moral approval on Hitler's regime, and more importantly that Hitler would have made any concession to maintain that approval.

Hitler wanted the concordat to give his regime legitimacy in the eyes of Germany's Catholics. Beyond that he had no intention of honoring it when it conflicted with his needs. The Vatican wanted the concordat for entirely different reasons—primarily to protect German Catholics in a political situation in which their traditional protector, the Catholic Center Party, no longer existed. It also gave the Pope a formal vehicle for protesting ill-treatment of the Church and Catholics. But the Vatican's role,

1. On the German bishops and their relations with the regime, see Repgen, 197–226.

and Pacelli's, in the demise of the Center Party are still hotly debated. Cornwell, citing German historian Klaus Scholder, claims that Pacelli torpedoed the Center Party in order to make an unholy alliance with Hitler, and that the Vatican hastened to sign the concordat as a means of consolidating its control over the German Church, part of Pacelli's life-long effort to do away with the independence of national churches. Cornwell further claims that that the triumph of Pacelli's policy deflated the German clergy's nascent opposition to the Nazi regime.[2] The issue is not that simple, and there are historians who argue the opposing view, that the dissolution of the Center Party was inevitable, that the Vatican had no role in its demise, and that the German bishops were not all that independent in any event.[3]

Pope Pius XI, during his pontificate from 1922 to 1939, faced a unique situation in his dealings with foreign governments. The end of World War I had seen the establishment of a number of new states, mainly in central and eastern Europe. He wanted to protect the Church in these countries, and the means for doing so was by concordats to regularize relations. Typically a concordat provided for some sort of state recognition of Catholic education, usually the Catholic religion taught in the state schools if the country was a majority Catholic country, and perhaps some sort of state funding for Catholic schools, whether majority or not. It also provided for recognition of the rights and privileges of the clergy—exemption from military duty or, at minimum, service in the medical corps, and exemption from taxation—along with recognition of sacramental marriage and other traditional church privileges. In return most concordats gave the state some privileges in the naming of the higher clergy, usu-

2. *Hitler's Pope*, 131–51

3. See the controversy explained in W. R. Ward, "Guilt and Innocence: The German Churches in the Twentieth Century," *Journal of Modern History* 68 (June 1996): 421–22; and also Stewart A. Stehlin, *Weimar and the Vatican 1919–1933* (Princeton: Princeton University Press, 1983), 435–36.

ally a right of veto of the Holy See's choice, or at least a right to nominate to the position.

During his pontificate, Pius XI had concluded more than thirty concordats. His two secretaries of state were Cardinal Pietro Gasparri to 1930, and Cardinal Eugenio Pacelli from 1930 until 1939, when Pacelli succeeded to the papacy as Pius XII. As a trained diplomat, Pacelli was well-versed in concordatory negotiations. As nuncio to Bavaria and Germany in the 1920s he had negotiated the Bavarian and Prussian concordats. He had tried to negotiate a concordat with the national government, but the Weimar regime had rejected his proposals.

When Hitler became chancellor in January 1933, he set out to establish complete control over Germany. One obstacle was the German bishops, who had repeatedly condemned the pagan ideas of Nazism; the other obstacle was the Center Party, the political arm of the German Church, established in the nineteenth century to fight Bismarck's Kulturkampf. Hitler won both over by promising to respect the rights of the Church, by emphasizing the centrality of Christianity to a revived Germany, and by promising to defend Germany against Bolshevism. The leader of the Center Party gave in and agreed to support Hitler's Enabling Act, which gave Hitler constitutional power to set up a totalitarian regime. Pius' critics argue that the Vatican urged the Center Party leaders to give in so that a concordat could be negotiated. His defenders contend that the Center Party had no chance against Hitler's Nazis in any event, and the wisest course was for the Centrists to avoid any activity that would prevent the signing of a concordat. Shortly after Hitler became Chancellor, Cardinal Michael Faulhaber of Munich went to Rome and returned to tell his episcopal brethren that Pope Pius XI approved of Hitler's anti-Bolshevism.[4] The bishops' opposition to Hitler faded. Into this situation Hitler sent Franz von Papen to Rome

4. Lewy, 30–31.

to negotiate a concordat. Hitler conceded everything that the Weimar government had not, and Pius XI directed Pacelli to negotiate for the Holy See.

By the time the negotiations began in earnest in June 1933, the Center Party's position had deteriorated to the point that the Vatican could no longer use it as a bargaining point. Thus, the pressure was on Pacelli to conclude a pact that would protect the Church, given that the Center party no longer had power. All of these negotiations were taking place in the midst of news from Germany that clergy and laity were being arrested and persecuted by the regime. Pacelli and Pius XI made the end of persecution a condition for signing the concordat.

One sticking point in the negotiations was the question of lay organizations and associations; the Nazi regime wanted a ban on those that were involved in political activity. This created an impasse over the definition of political activity until the negotiators agreed to draw up a list of protected organizations in the future.

The final version of the concordat provided for continued state subsidization of the Church, religious instruction "in accord with the principles of the Catholic Church" in all public schools, and a guarantee of the continued existence of Catholic schools (this provision was especially welcomed by the hierarchy, which had long hoped to see the government provide for the legal equality of church schools with interdenominational schools). It obliged the Holy See to inform the government of its intended episcopal appointments to ensure that there was no political opposition to the nominees. It also stipulated that the clergy refrain from political activity. A secret annex provided for the exemption from conscription of all clergy and seminarians.[5]

5. See the excellent commentary by Joseph A. Biesinger, "The Reich Concordat of 1933," in *Controversial Concordats*, ed. Frank J. Coppa (Washington: The Catholic University of America Press, 1999), 120–81; see pp. 205–14 for the text of the concordat.

As soon as the concordat was signed, Hitler hailed it as a great achievement, the Vatican's "recognition of the present government," and he played this propaganda issue, thereby making the concordat more than it was, i.e., the Church's approval of the Nazi regime. On the other hand, the Vatican got what it had wanted for years, namely a guarantee of freedom of Catholic education. Pacelli, in two articles in *L'Osservatore Romano*, said that Hitler's claim that the Church now approved of Nazism was absolutely wrong. All the Church had done was to negotiate a treaty, nothing more, and it implied no judgment on the nature of the regime. Furthermore, the new code of canon law was recognized as one of the provisions of the concordat, and this was a great concession to the Church, Pacelli said.[6]

Pacelli confided to Ivone Kirkpatrick, the British minister to the Holy See, that he really had no choice but to sign. Kirkpatrick cabled London that Pacelli had said, "A pistol had been pointed at his head and he had no alternative. . . . Not only that, but he was given no more than a week to make up his mind [and] it was a case of then or never. . . . The spiritual welfare of 20 million Catholic souls in Germany was at stake and that was the first and, indeed, the only consideration," and "he had to choose between an agreement on [Nazi] lines and the virtual elimination of the Catholic Church in the Reich."[7] Scholder says that, while the Vatican was under great pressure to conclude a concordat—given the loss of its bargaining chip, the Center Party—Pacelli knew that Hitler was also under pressure to have a concordat as a means of getting world recognition of his regime. Pacelli, he says, should have held out for greater clarity

6. *L'Osservatore Romano*, July 26 and 27, 1933. See Klaus Scholder, *The Churches and the Third Reich*, 1:407.

7. Kirkpatrick to Sir Robert Vansittart, 19 August 1933, *Documents on British Foreign Policy, 1919–1939*, 2d Series (London: Her Majesty's Stationery Office, 1956), 5:524–55.

on the issue of lay associations. According to Scholder, the final result was—against Church intentions—the approval of the Nazi regime in the eyes of Catholics in Germany and the world in general.[8] But it is difficult to blame Pacelli for the image that the concordat had in the eyes of Catholics or the world. True, as chief negotiator for the Pope, Pacelli had some leeway, and presumably some influence on the Pope. He was not, however, the pope. Pius XI had definite views on Germany, and he disapproved of Catholic parties in general. The Germans had proposed the concordat. To have rejected it out of hand would have been prejudicial to the rights of Catholics in Germany. Would Hitler have attacked them if the concordat had been rejected? He had already arrested many laypersons. Would he have risked a Vatican condemnation at this early point in his rule? What could the Pope have done in any event? He could condemn the regime's persecution of Catholics, something the German bishops had already done. The prudent thing to do—and Pacelli was always most prudent—was to get concessions from the regime and let the propaganda chips fall where they might.

John Conway says, "The conclusion of the Reich Concordat with the new Nazi regime in 1933 is therefore not to be seen as a sign of the Vatican's approval . . . but rather as an attempt to control [the regime's] unpredictable revolutionary fervor within some legally binding framework." At the same time, "the criticism is valid that the concordat . . . made it impossible for the German Catholics to organize a politically effective campaign against the Nazi state, or even to admit that their evaluation of the new regime's intentions had been faulty."[9] Perhaps the most succinct defense of the Pope and Pacelli is that of the German historian Konrad Repgen, who says that for the Church, the

8. Scholder, 381ff.
9. "The Vatican, Germany and the Holocaust," 106–7.

concordat "was not an alliance but an instrument of defense."[10]

Even many German Jews were unclear as to the Nazi regime's intentions. Saul Friedlander, in a later work, points out that in 1933 many Jews did not expect a rigid persecution. Many Germans still shopped at Jewish stores even after a boycott was announced. Some Jews even supported the Nazis as a movement toward national regeneration.[11] With this consideration, to expect Catholics to have had the foresight to see the Holocaust as the eventual result of their support of the regime appears to be unrealistic.

Once put into effect, the concordat was violated within a year by Hitler, and Pacelli began a long series of diplomatic protests that lasted throughout his tenure as Secretary of State. When he became Pope, did the maintenance of the concordat influence his decision to avoid public criticism of the Nazi government? He expressed his fears for German Catholics to Domenico Tardini, his Subsecretary of State: when the French government asked in late August 1939 for a papal statement in support of Poland in the last days of negotiation before war broke out, Pius told Tardini, "We should not forget that in the Reich there are 40,000,000 [*sic*] Catholics. To what might they not be exposed after such action by the Holy See!"[12] On the other hand, Carlo Falconi says that the issuance of Pius XI's encyclical *Mit Brennender Sorge* gave the Nazi regime ample reason to abrogate the concordat unilaterally, and it did not do so. Presumably, he says, Hitler would not abrogate the concordat under continued criticism.[13] Hitler talked in 1942 about "settling accounts" with the Church once the war was over, but he hesitated to take any ac-

10. "German Catholicism," 205.

11. Saul Friedlander, *Nazi Germany and the Jews: The Years of Persecution, 1933–1939* (New York: HarperCollins, 1997), 14–17.

12. 28 August 1939, *ADSS* 1:240.

13. *Silence*, 78.

tion as long as the war continued and he needed the support of Germany's Catholics.[14] Did the Pope know this? It seems logical that he would have had some inkling of Hitler's hesitation, and he would at the same time have realized that Hitler could abrogate the concordat any time he wished. The prudent thing to do would be to avoid provocation. In his 1945 justification of his policy toward Germany, Pius said that "the concordat brought some advantages, or at least prevented worse evils. In fact, despite all the violations to which it was subjected the concordat gave Catholics a juridical basis for their defense, a stronghold behind which to shield themselves in their opposition, so long as this was possible, to the rising tide of religious persecution."[15] Considering all of the reasons for the Pope's behavior, his fear of Hitler's breaking the concordat was probably a reason, but not as strong an explanation as other ones.

14. *Hitler's Secret Conversations*, 449–551.
15. Cited in *The Tablet*, 9 June 1945, 268.

Chapter 7

Vatican Diplomacy Has Always Been Cautious

It has been argued by Pius' defenders that he was simply following papal tradition in exercising a cautious diplomatic policy during World War II, and in doing so he was, as Victor Conzemius says, "the victim of his own training, of the juridical structure of Catholicism, and of the existing conventions of accords between church and state."[1] Conzemius goes on to argue that the problem with Pius was not his silence, but rather the efficacy of his diplomacy. This insightful observation brings up the question of the effectiveness of papal diplomacy in general.

Diplomacy has a different and a wider meaning for the Holy See than it does for nations. Traditionally the term has meant the method of conducting foreign relations. In the context of a nation, it is fairly easy to distinguish between foreign and domestic relations. But the Holy See is an international institution and even the internal workings of the Church have an impact everywhere there are Catholics. Whatever the Pope says in public has an impact outside of the Vatican. Such statements become matters of

1. "Le Saint–Siège," 472.

diplomatic concern when the pope instructs Catholics on issues on which the state has a definite policy. Thus, a papal instruction on a purely disciplinary matter—the ordination of women, for example—is of no concern to the state, because the state has no policy toward such a matter. But on policies concerning marriage—a sacrament in the eyes of the Church—the state has a very definite interest, because marriage is also a civil affair, determining inheritance rights and other matters. Then there are those issues that appear to have no secular concern, but which, in fact, do.

Consider, for example, the canonization of a saint. This would appear to be a matter important only for the faithful and to have no effect upon a foreign government. Yet, it does have an impact. In 1920, Pope Benedict XV canonized Joan of Arc, 400 years after her death. This had political significance, for it happened when the papacy was attempting to regularize relations with France after the turmoil of the French anticlerical laws and the separation of church and state earlier in the century. Aside from its religious significance, the canonization was a goodwill offering to the French government, and diplomatic relations were resumed in 1924 after having been broken off in 1904.

Pius was a trained diplomat and he knew the limits of papal diplomacy. The Vatican is a small state and cautious diplomacy is a sensible policy for any small state and particularly for one without any means to defend itself. Paradoxically, however, that very weakness of the papacy can translate into moral power, for the Holy See appears to have no pretensions to material power. But the problem is that the Catholic Church, throughout the world, is not simply a spiritual institution. It has a number of material needs and demands: its clergy need protection and usually dispensation from certain civic duties, such as military conscription; it needs schools and therefore academic protection; it needs buildings and property to maintain itself. Where these exist, as they did in Germany and in its satellite and occupied states during World War II, then this concern with material needs puts a brake upon the moral power of the Church. Pius' diplomacy reflected this concern.

John Morley, in his study of Vatican diplomacy, says that diplomacy "was the principal instrument used by the Catholic Church in attempting to exert its moral authority during the Second World War."[2] There were other choices, he continues, but Pius chose diplomacy. What were these other choices? Covert activity was one—for example, the private order given by the Pope to various clergy and religious to open their doors to the victims of Nazi terror. This was apparently done, but Morley contends it was not the *principal* activity of the Holy See. Furthermore, he says that Pius' reliance on traditional diplomatic practice based on reserve and prudence "could not coexist with humanitarian concern."[3]

While it would appear, then, that Vatican diplomacy has usually been cautious in modern times, in fact, much has depended on the circumstances. Nineteenth-century popes were often confrontational, especially through the pontificate of Pius IX. Preserving the independence of the Papal States and Rome was one of their major concerns, and none was loath to condemn the forces of Italian unification, or the new Italian state after 1860. Popes have always condemned legislation against the Church: some have done so more quietly, through diplomatic channels and mildly worded public statements, while others have issued vigorous broadsides against erring states. Leo XIII (1878–1903) was a cautious diplomat, as was Benedict XV (1914–1922), but Pius X (1903–1914) and Pius XI (1922–1939) were more outspoken, protesting what they considered the anti-Catholic and anti-Christian practices of governments everywhere.

2. *Vatican Diplomacy*, 6.
3. *Vatican Diplomacy*, 208.

The issue for Pius XII was complicated by the question of human rights and injustice to all people, not only Catholics. When he was papal Secretary of State, he protested the Nazi regime's violations of the Reich Concordat of 1933 through diplomatic means, while the Pope, Pius XI, made a forceful protest in his encyclical, *Mit Brennender Sorge*. When Pius XII became pope and the war began, the Nazi regime eased its attacks upon the Church in Germany, but it began a wholesale persecution of people everywhere in the occupied countries.

At this juncture, Pius changed from his predecessor's confrontational tactics to a stance of quiet diplomacy. One of the issues raised by Pius' critics is his cancellation of plans to publish his predecessor's unfinished encyclical, *Humani Generis Unitas*. This work, commissioned by Pius XI, condemned anti-Semitism and racism. Pius XII shelved the unedited draft when he became pope because he apparently believed that his diplomacy would have a better chance of success without such a provocative declaration; his defenders argue that many of the same ideas (although in less forceful language) from the unpublished encyclical can be found in Pius XII's first encyclical *Summi Pontificatus*, published shortly after he became pope.[4]

The new Pope's diplomacy did not mean an end to Vatican complaints. Pius' nuncio to Berlin, Cesare Orsenigo, was instructed to protest the persecution of Poland's Catholics, but the German government responded that his jurisdiction did not extend to Poland. Hence, the dilemma for Pius. His quiet diplomacy was not working, so he was faced with the choice of continuing to try to make it effective, or of publicly protesting German actions. He chose the former, apparently because he believed that public protests would only make things worse.

4. See Frank J. Coppa, "The Hidden Encyclical of Pius XI against Racism and Anti-Semitism Uncovered—Once Again!" *Catholic Historical Review* 84, no. 1 (January 1998): 63–72.

In the German satellite states, he instructed his nuncios to use their diplomatic skills to protest violations of both Catholic and human rights. Italy was a different case. The popes always had more political power in Italy than elsewhere by virtue of their position as Bishops of Rome and Primates of Italy. But this power tended to vary in proportion to the power of the leaders of the Italian state. Papal prestige and therefore political power in Italy grew as the power of the Italian leaders weakened. This began to happen after Mussolini took Italy into the war in 1940 on Hitler's side. The Italian people were generally opposed to the war, and the monarchy was hesitant to oppose Mussolini. Italians began to look to Pope Pius for leadership, but the Lateran Treaty forbade such activity, nor did the Vatican have the machinery to step in.

In the few weeks between the fall of Mussolini in July 1943 and the Allied invasion in September, the King and Marshal Pietro Badoglio governed; then, with the Allied invasion, the Germans came to dominate Rome and northern Italy. During this chaotic period, the Pope was concerned primarily with Italian events in order to maintain the independence and integrity of the Holy See. These events dictated a cautious policy of not antagonizing the German occupiers in the months from September 1943 to June 1944.

After the war ended in 1945, there was a change in Pius' diplomacy. He became outspoken in his protests against Communist governments' restrictions upon Catholics, and in 1949 he decreed excommunication for those Catholics who joined the Communist Party.[5] In Italy, he forbade Italian Catholics, under pain of excommunication, to support Communist candidates in the parliamentary elections of 1948. He condemned the Soviet

5. Jonathan Luxmoore and Jolanta Babiuch, *The Vatican and the Red Flag: The Struggle for the Soul of Eastern Europe* (London: Geoffrey Chapman, 1999), 65.

invasion of Hungary in 1956. In view of these outspoken public protests, why did Pius not forcefully condemn Nazi Germany?

The difference appears to be that the Nazi regime, during the war, was not persecuting Catholics as Catholics. Hundreds of priests and laymen were imprisoned because of their overt or perceived opposition to the regime, but the great mass of Catholics were free to practice their faith. A protest could make things worse. In the Soviet satellites after 1945, all Catholics came under proscriptive measures, and there were limitations on the practice of their faith everywhere. Thus, a protest might do some good. Except in rare instances, papal diplomacy with Communists accomplished little. Moreover, Pius was concerned that Catholics might join schismatic churches organized by the Communist governments. Because his diplomacy was ineffective with the governments, he appealed to the masses of Catholics in those countries. And in Italy, there was no fear of persecution, so the Pope was free to say what he wished.

The Italian historian Giovanni Miccoli, in his analysis of the Vatican's wartime policy, says that the mind-set of the Vatican was anachronistic: that Pius and his officials thought in terms of medieval notions of a just war, and as a result papal protests were general rather than specific. The Pope, he says, could not give the precise answers to the horrors he was dealing with because he was tied to anachronistic formulations; and that even when he did remonstrate, these formulations kept his protests from being forceful.[6]

Pius XII practiced cautious diplomacy against the Nazi government during the war; but he did not do so at all times, as witness his secretly agreeing to serve as a conduit for negotiations between anti-Nazi Germans and the British government shortly

6. Miccoli, *I dilemmi*, 406, 412–13.

after the war broke out. And, he was not cautious against Communist governments during the Cold War. The circumstances of World War II called for unusual behavior on the part of the papacy. Pius believed that he could not condemn forcefully with impunity. Perhaps another pope might have acted differently; certainly it would have taken a pope with a different training and personality to do the unusual. Pius was not that pope.

Chapter 8

A Crisis of Conscience for German Catholics

One of the strongest arguments critics have made is that Pius did not protest against the Nazi terror because such a protest would have caused a crisis of conscience for German Catholics, forcing them to choose between their church and their state, and Pius did not want to take this risk for two reasons. If Germany's Catholics responded to support a papal protest, then they would have had to face the overwhelmingly coercive power of the state. If they did not, then it would be a shattering blow to the Pope's prestige, but worse, it would cause a falling away from the Church of millions of Catholics.[1]

The Pope's detractors say that he should have made such a protest whatever the consequences because it was the right and moral thing to do. They compare him unfavorably with his predecessor, Pius XI, who condemned Nazi racism and the worship of the state in his 1937 encyclical, *Mit Brennender Sorge*. Pius XI, they argue, was not concerned about the effect that his condemnation would

---

1. Zuccotti, 311, is most forceful on this issue.

have upon German Catholics.[2] As for the fear of a schism—that those Catholics would not obey the Pope—critics can argue that popes had never taken such factors into account in the past, that they had condemned liberalism, modernism, socialism, communism, religious liberty, and other ideologies without regard to the number of faithful whom they might have alienated. Furthermore, if all German Catholics were to heed the Pope and refuse to support the Nazi regime, then that regime would have collapsed, for Catholics made up some forty percent of the German population. No state could survive with that many people actively opposed to it; certainly the German armies could not have held out against the Allies if they could not have counted on the support of the Catholics in their ranks.

Is there any solid evidence that Pius considered the German conscience in his approach to the problem of German terror? The most oft-cited statement is that advanced by an Italian journalist, Edoardo Senatra, who was "on friendly terms with Pius XII," according to the Berlin *Petrusblatt.* In a conference at the Jewish Gemeindehaus in Berlin on March 11, 1963, Senatra said that during the war he asked Pius about protesting the destruction of the Jews, and Pius answered, "Dear friend, do not forget that millions of Catholics serve in the German armies. Shall I bring them into conflicts of conscience? They have taken an oath, they owe obedience."[3] The problem with quotes such as these is that they are most difficult to verify. There is, as far as I know, no independent verification of Senatra's statement. Fur-

2. Zuccotti, 21–23, 40, differs from most critics of Pius XII by criticizing Pius XI as well, pointing out that he did not protest the Nazi terror which had already begun in Germany while he was Pope; and that *Mit Brenender Sorge* was not aimed at the German terror but rather at the German government's violation of the concordat.

3. Quoted in Otto Kohler, "Der Streit um den Stellvertreter," published in *Frankfurter Hefte,* May 1963, in Fritz J. Raddatz, ed., *Summa Iniuria oder Durfte der Papst schweigen?* (Hamburg: Rowohlt, 1964), 223.

thermore, it appears out of keeping with Pius' character. There is no other evidence that he spoke frankly with reporters. Pius was a trained diplomat, not given to off-the-cuff remarks of this sort. It seems hardly likely that Pius would value the oath the German soldiers took to obey Hitler above their consciences. W. A. Purdy says, "If Pius indeed uttered [the words about obedience], it is hard to understand how he, an expert canon lawyer, could have done so if he really knew what was going on in Germany."[4]

But historian Michael Marrus says that the threat of a German schism was a consideration in Pius' approach.[5] And Guenter Lewy uses Senatra's statement to bolster his contention that it was so. He says, "The Pope knew that the German Catholics were not prepared to suffer martyrdom for their Church; still less were they willing to incur the wrath of their Nazi rulers for the sake of the Jews whom their own bishops for years had castigated as a harmful influence in German life."[6] Gordon Zahn, the author of the influential study *German Catholics and Hitler's Wars,* a substantial criticism of the German bishops, says no papal denunciation "no matter how strong in tone and specific in terms, would have succeeded in rallying the general Catholic population to prospective martyrdom." Most German Catholics "would not have dared nor wished to turn against their nation's leaders."[7]

The problem of the German bishops must also be looked at in this regard. Most were patriotic Germans supporting the war effort. Would they have supported the Pope in such a protest? Would any have objected and started a schismatic church? After

---

4. *The Church on the Move* (London: Hollis and Carter, 1966), 260. See also the discussion in Jacques Nobécourt, *"Le Vicaire" et l'Histoire,* 245.

5. *The Holocaust in History,* 184.

6. *Catholic Church,* 304.

7. "Catholic Responses to the Holocaust," *Thought* 56 (June 1981): 158.

all, the only schismatic church of any size in recent history was a German one, started in protest against the dogma of papal infallibility. This would certainly have been an element in Pius' thinking on the subject. He had been warned on this point: shortly after his election, in March 1939, Cardinal Faulhaber had mentioned the threat of a German National Church, sponsored by the Nazi regime.[8] Perhaps the Pope believed that one reason the German bishops did not speak out forcefully for the Jews was that Catholics themselves had been persecuted in Germany and they did not want to expend their capital on protecting someone else while they were under attack.[9]

The Italian historian Alberto Giovannetti, one of the first writers on the topic, defends Pius by saying that an interdict would "merely put 30 million [*sic*] German Catholics in a dilemma of conscience, in which they must either obey the Church and risk death . . . or obey the State and sustain a schism, equally to the ruin of Catholicism in Germany."[10] Donald J. Dietrich also says that Germans would probably have refused to understand a papal condemnation or to respond to papal leadership.[11] John Conway argues that German Catholics were "infected" with anti-Semitism and "would have refused to understand, let alone to respond to, any leadership from the Pope."[12] He furthermore argues that Vatican power was continually being eroded and that the Pope feared a loss of credibility if he made a protest and it went unheeded.[13] Pierre Blet says that Pius was afraid that a

8. 5 March 1939, *ADSS* 2:400–401.

9. This argument is implied in Repgen, 214.

10. *L'Action du Vatican*, 116.

11. "Historical Judgments and Eternal Verities," *Society* 20, no. 3 (1983): 31–35.

12. "The Silence of Pope Pius XII," *Review of Politics* 27, no. 1 (January 1965): 128.

13. "Catholicism and the Jews during the Nazi Period and After," in *Judaism and Christianity under the Impact of National Socialism*, ed. Otto Dov Kulka and Paul R. Mendes-Flohr, 447.

public protest from the Pope would be transformed by Nazi propagandist Josef Goebbels into an attack on German Catholics and thereby turn them against the Pope and the Church.[14] There was a precedent for such fear: the German propaganda services had changed Pius' message of sympathy for the Poles in his encyclical *Summi Pontificatus* and had interpreted it in such a way as to support German aims.[15]

Finally, Beata Ruhm von Oppen, one of the most trenchant critics of Pius' detractors, and one of the most profound in her insights, notes that in 1940, the Pope's nuncio in Berlin, Cesare Orsenigo, sent a message to Pius. Orsenigo wrote that he feared mass apostasy of German Catholics, "unless the clergy appeased the regime and relieved members of the church of a conflict of conscience to which they were not equal." Thus, she points to the absurdity of the critics' claim that if the Pope had spoken out, German Catholics would have followed him against Hitler.[16]

The Nazi regime commanded an immensely powerful state. Most Germans, whatever their religion, if put to the test would choose their state over their church because it was the more immediately powerful of the two. It is a fact of modern life, historian John Lukacs perceptively notes, that, as in nations everywhere, "a German Catholic thought of himself as a German who happened to be Catholic, not the reverse."[17] For the Pope to have asked German Catholics to oppose the brutal Nazi regime would have been for him to ask for heroic resistance on the part of the people; and while there are instances of Christians who resisted the regime, they paid for it with their lives. The mass of people were not capable of such heroic action.

Furthermore, the argument that popes in the past never hesi-

14. *Pie XII*, 322.

15. Chadwick, *Britain and the Vatican*, 85.

16. "Nazis and Christians," 406.

17. *The Last European War* (Garden City, N.Y.: Anchor Press/Doubleday, 1976), 456.

tated to condemn ideologies that they believed were harmful ignores the fact that none of those ideologies threatened the faithful in the way the power of a state could. If Catholics followed the papal admonitions and stood against religious liberty, or liberalism, they would not have been persecuted or called to task by the state for their views, because the state, by its very nature, would be a liberal state if it propounded these positions; its defense of civil rights would be at the heart of its being. If Catholics opposed the Nazi regime, they could be imprisoned or even executed—as some were—because the Nazi state was not a liberal state.

It appears then, that if such a consideration—namely that Pius did not want to create a crisis of conscience for German Catholics—was in fact a reason why he did not make a strong protest, then it must also be said that Pius must have judged that the Germans would not be up to the standard of martyrdom, which such a protest might have led to. Such a rational calculation appears to have been a substantial factor in Pius' behavior, but it appears that other considerations weighed more heavily.

During the war, the American chargé at the Vatican, Harold Tittmann, said in a dispatch to Washington that he believed that "another motive, possibly the controlling one, behind the Pope's disinclination to denounce Nazi atrocities is his fear that if he does so now, the German people, in the bitterness of their defeat, will reproach him later on for having contributed, if only indirectly, to this defeat."[18] None of Pius' detractors or defenders has accepted Tittmann's assessment as a sound reason for Pius' course of action.

18. *FRUS*, 6 October 1942, 3:777.

Chapter 9

Pius Feared Communism
More than Nazism

One of the most widely believed arguments about Pius and his alleged silence is that he viewed Communism as the greatest threat to Christian Europe and therefore saw Germany as a bulwark against the expansion of Soviet Communism. This is the central argument that Saul Friedlander makes. Acknowledging that he did not have all of the documents at his disposal at the time he wrote, Friedlander says that the German documents show that "Pius XII feared a Bolshevization of Europe more than anything else and hoped, it seems, that Hitler [*sic*] Germany, if it were eventually reconciled with the Western Allies, would become the essential rampart against any advance by the Soviet Union toward the West."[1]

Among the arguments advanced to bolster this thesis is the experience Pius had when he was nuncio to Bavaria in 1919, at the end of World War I when German Communists took over the government of Bavaria and he was threatened by revolutionaries. According to the story, he

1. *Pius XII*, 236.

faced them down but was left with a lifelong dislike of Communism and all leftist movements.

While this incident may have contributed to his aversion to Communism, there is no doubt that Pius, along with most clergy in the world, feared the spread of Communism under any circumstance. It was, after all, avowedly atheistic and, at least in its Soviet phase, determined to destroy religion in all of its aspects. Pius did not need the Bavarian experience to cause his fear. Pius' most devoted hagiographer, Michael O'Carroll, rejects this notion with the comment that this is "a strange suggestion about a man with a worldwide outlook and a habit of basing judgement only on the fullest evidence available."[2]

Critics frequently overlook the Spanish Civil War as a determining factor in the clergy's fear of Communism. In the summer and fall of 1936, when Pius, as Cardinal Pacelli, was Secretary of State and concerned with German violations of the concordat, Spanish leftist agitators were killing nearly seven thousand priests and religious. These leftists were not Communists, for Soviet policy toward Spain was to stress moderation; but for the Vatican, as well as for the world in general, no distinction was made between Communists, anarchists, or other proletarian revolutionaries. The fact was that clergy and practicing Catholics were being killed in numbers not seen in the West since the persecutions of the Roman Empire.

Pacelli handled the diplomatic exchanges with the Spanish Republican Government, which wanted to stop this anticlerical fury. Pope Pius XI condemned the fury in an encyclical on Communism, *Divini Redemptoris*, which was issued in the same month, March 1937, as *Mit Brennender Sorge*. There is no question that this savage fury loomed large in Pius XII's mind when he

2. *Pius XII: Greatness Dishonoured* (Chicago: Franciscan Herald Press, 1980), 30.

contemplated the balance of power and the actions of the Soviets and Germans once he became pope.

What was his view of the Soviet-German non-aggression pact of August 1939, which not only enabled Hitler to invade western Poland, but also allowed the Soviets to invade eastern Poland without fear of a conflict with Germany? It would be difficult for any educated observer, much less the experienced diplomat Pius, to see in the pact and the subsequent invasion anything more than a cynical violation of all of Hitler's anti-Communist rhetoric. How could such an action, which turned half of Poland over to the Soviets, justify supporting Germany as a bulwark of the Christian west?

The documents that Freidlander uses to justify his conclusion that Pius was silent because he favored Germany as a bulwark against Soviet expansion are those of the Germans. German Foreign Minister Joachim von Ribbentrop visited Pius in March 1940; in Ribbentrop's memorandum of the conversation, Friedlander finds evidence that the Pope supported Germany's position as bulwark against Soviet expansion, while at the same time indicating his opposition to the Soviet-German non-aggression pact.[3] Later, when Germany attacked the Soviet Union in June 1941, German diplomats made an effort to get the Pope to declare this struggle as a crusade. It failed, for Pius would have nothing to do with such an idea. However, there were Italian clergy who hailed the invasion of Russia as a crusade (so reported Fritz Menshausen, the German chargé at the Vatican, to his superiors in Berlin). Menshausen also believed that "in his heart, so runs the constantly reiterated assurance, Pius XII is on the side of the Axis Powers."[4] Friedlander also cites Ernst von Weizsäcker, the German Foreign Office permanent undersecre-

3. *Pius XII*, 41–47.
4. Cited in Friedlander, *Pius XII*, 84.

tary (before he became Ambassador to the Holy See), in October 1941, who reported that the Spanish Ambassador to Berlin noted in a conversation with the nuncio in Madrid that Pius "had friendly feelings for the Reich. He had no more ardent wish for the Führer than to see him gain a victory over Bolshevism."[5]

All of these documents have been challenged as written by self-serving Germans who used them for their own ends. Conway points out that Friedlander wrote his book before the Vatican documents were released, and they do not back up his claim.[6] He says, "It is quite erroneous to suggest that there was any sympathy for or support of the Nazis, even as a bulwark against the equally loathed Bolsheviks."[7] Owen Chadwick, in his review of the Vatican documents agrees: Pius "thought it permissible to resist German aggression even with the aid of a Russian alliance, and was prepared for political measures to that end where such measures were possible."[8]

Pius' authorization of a letter from Secretary of State Maglione to the Apostolic Delegate in Washington lends support to this interpretation. The American bishops had been concerned about President Franklin Roosevelt's extension of Lend-Lease aid to the Soviet Union after the German attack in the summer of 1941; they cited the condemnation by Pius XI in his 1937 encyclical, *Divini Redemptoris,* of any aid given to Communists. Maglione's letter eased this fear by making a distinction between the Communist government and the people of the Soviet Union. It was permissible, he said, to aid the latter.[9]

5. Cited in Friedlander, *Pius XII,* 85.

6. "The Meeting between Pope Pius XII and Ribbentrop," *Historical Papers of the Canadian Historical Association* 1 (1968): 217.

7. "The Vatican, Germany and the Holocaust," 106.

8. In a review of volume 5 of *ADSS* in the *Journal of Ecclesiastical History* 21, no. 3 (1970):279–80.

9. 20 September 1941, *ADSS* 5:240–41.

Pius' German advisor, Jesuit Robert Lieber, clarifies the issue from his first-hand knowledge of the Pope. By 1943, he says, "of the two systems, Nazism and Bolshevism, Pius looked far into the future and considered Bolshevism the more dangerous," because with an impending German defeat, Nazism was finished as an ideology, while Bolshevism was growing in strength and was a danger for the future of Europe.[10]

Finally, Friedlander himself admits that his conclusion—that Pius' fear of the Bolshevisation of Europe was a major factor in his silence—has not been firmly established: "Obviously, this is no more than a hypothesis which no text explicitly proves."[11]

Considering all of these documents and views of historians, it appears that the reason advanced, primarily by Friedlander, and then taken back by Friedlander, is not justified. Despite Pius' admiration of German culture and his solicitude for German Catholics, he never saw Germany, under Nazism, as a bulwark of Western Christianity against the advance of Bolshevism from the Soviet Union. What it appears he hoped for was the overthrow of the Nazi regime and its replacement by a government that rejected the Nazi ideology; such a government could win his support, and that, presumably, is the reason he decided to serve as a conduit and guarantor between anti-Nazi conspirators and the British government shortly after the war began in 1939. Whether he would have supported such a government in all circumstances is another question which cannot be answered.

10. Robert Lieber, "Der Papst and die Verfolgung der Juden," in *Summa Inuria oder Durfte der Papst schweigen?* ed. Fritz J. Raddatz (Hamburg: Rowohlt, 1964), 104.

11. *Pius XII*, 134.

Chapter 10

Pius Wanted to Serve as
Mediator in the War

From he time of the loss of the Papal States in 1871, the papacy attempted to play a role in mediating conflicts between states. Leo XIII arbitrated a conflict between Germany and Spain in 1885 over possession of the Caroline Islands, thereby raising the international prestige of the papacy. During World War I, the Holy See followed a policy of neutrality in the hope of mediating the struggle.[1] In 1917 Pope Benedict XV offered a plan to end the conflict, but the Allies claimed his plan favored the Central Powers. Nonetheless, the precedent was established, and the young Pacelli, as nuncio to Bavaria, carried Benedict's messages to the Kaiser.

In the summer of 1939 Pius tried to prevent the war by offering his services to mediate the problems, even to the extent of urging Poland to give in to Germany's demands for the Polish Corridor and Danzig. None of the powers was interested in papal mediation, the Germans because

1. See the scholarly study by John Pollard, *The Unknown Pope: Benedict XV* (London: Geoffrey Chapman, 1999), 85ff.

they wanted more of Poland, and the Poles and the Western Allies because they did not want German domination of Poland.

After the fall of Poland at the end of September 1939, Pius apparently believed that the war was over, that the Allies and Germany would get together to conclude a peace treaty, and further that the belligerents would ask for his mediation. In order to mediate, Pius had to remain absolutely neutral, which meant, he believed, that he could not criticize either belligerent. It has been argued that this, along with the traditional policy of maintaining papal neutrality in wars with large numbers of Catholics on both sides, is one reason he did not condemn the German invasion. By the end of October, his services had not been requested, and he began to implicitly criticize the Germans in his encyclical *Summi Pontificatus* and in his Christmas message of December 1939. The criticism was implicit in order to preserve his neutrality so that he could still serve as a trustworthy mediator. At the same time, however, he was covertly engaged as a conduit between the German opposition to Hitler and the British Government, and more: he promised he would serve as a guarantor of whatever plan was worked out by the conspirators.[2] The German government never found out about Pius' clandestine activities. In any event, the conspiracy fell through, to the relief of the Pope's advisors.

Pius was surely disappointed that none of the belligerents asked for his mediation at any time during the war. Despite his intentions, the desire to serve as a mediator had an effect upon his willingness to protest German atrocities. According to David Alvarez in his well-documented study, "the commitment to one imperative, for example the need to remain an acceptable mediator, might compromise the satisfaction of another, such as the duty to provide moral leadership. These problems—the insuffi-

2. Deutsch, 121; and Chadwick, *Britain and the Vatican*, 86ff.

ciency of means and the complexity of ends—would frustrate Vatican diplomacy throughout the Second World War."[3]

There is no lack of documentation showing that Pius wanted to mediate the conflict. But mediation depended on the consent of the belligerents. In January 1943, Pius told the Hungarian premier, Nicholas Kállay, that the Holy See could not take the initiative to mediate the war. Only the belligerent powers could do so. He feared that if the Holy See made a peace proposal and it was accepted by one side, then the other side would reject the proposal and the result would be that the Holy See would then be seen as an ally of the power that accepted the proposal. The final result would be that the impartiality of the Church would be compromised.[4]

Was there ever an opportunity to mediate the conflict? In retrospect, it appears that Hitler was never interested in mediation, papal or otherwise; he was interested only in achieving his aim, which was the total subordination of his enemies. Nor were the Allies interested in mediation; there was to be no compromise with Hitler. Why could not the Pope have realized the nature of this conflict, with its commitment on both sides to total victory? Was Pius bemused by the papal experience of World War I, where mediation was distinctly possible?

On the other hand, with Germany on the defensive by 1943, did Pius continue to believe that Hitler might be open to mediation? If so, he misjudged the Allies' intentions, for they had no interest in compromising with Hitler. The German conspirators of the July 20, 1944, plot, believed that a compromise was possible with the Allies; they would assassinate Hitler and set up a government of national restoration and give up Germany's

3. "The Vatican and the Fall of Poland," in *The Opening of the Second World War*, ed. David W. Pike (New York: Peter Lang, 1991), 94.

4. Nicholas Kállay, *Hungarian Premier* (New York: Columbia University Press, 1954), 171.

gains. The Allies they contacted told them to go ahead, but said they could make no prior commitments. If the German conspirators accepted this proviso and went ahead with their plans, it is difficult to fault the Pope for making the same assumption—namely that a compromise was not out of the question.

Pius was a trained diplomat and he should have seen the possibilities and contingencies; on the other hand, there were other equally trained professionals who did not; furthermore, Pius' sources of information were not as great as is generally believed. However, seen in the context of the times, the chance that at any time Hitler might be overthrown and an anti-Nazi German government come to power could have made compromise seem likely. This possibility must have been a motive for Pius to keep the door open to mediation.

All historians agree that Pius wanted to mediate the war and therefore was less critical of the Germans than he should have been. John Conway says that the Pope feared that once denunciations of war crimes started, "it would be impossible to stop and would have to be extended to all violations of the moral and natural laws, however great or small." Such condemnations, he continues, would have required great care and accurate information and would have destroyed any hope of impartiality and therefore mediation.[5] Michael Marrus says that as time went on, Pius "clung to the wreckage of his prewar policy" of diplomatic mediation even when it no longer had a chance of success.[6] Susan Zuccotti says that the Pope "continued to nurse his illusions to the end," believing that the Germans would call upon his services "only if he demonstrated neutrality and good will."[7] Owen Chadwick puts the problem succinctly: "The condition of successful [mediation] was a reputation for fair-mindedness, gen-

5. "Vatican, Germany and the Holocaust," 109.
6. *The Holocaust in History*, 179–83.
7. Zuccotti, 314.

uine concern as a Christian pastor, and above all neutrality. Pius XII succeeded in achieving all this respect. But to achieve neutral status was not done without cost, and a cost which was to become greater as the war deteriorated. The cost was public silence, except in generalities."[8]

It should, however, be pointed out that Pius did not consider his policy one of indifference to the warring powers. He told Cardinal Faulhaber that his attitude was not one of neutrality, which he said was "passive indifference," but rather one of impartiality, "which judges according to truth and justice."[9] This is a subtle distinction that gets lost in the great moral issues of World War II.

Michael Phayer says that playing the role of mediator was one of the two chief reasons why Pius did not make a strong protest against the Germans, and that his purpose was to ensure that Germany remained strong against Communist Russia. Phayer claims that the Pope adhered to "strict diplomatic rules" when asked to denounce the Holocaust, but engaged in backstairs diplomacy to mediate an end to the war.[10]

Finally, Leonidas Hill says that the Pope wanted to maintain neutrality, not in order to mediate the war, but rather to preserve the unity of the Church: approving one of the belligerents would alienate Catholics on the other side.[11] This is an intriguing notion that would help explain why Pius maintained his neutrality long after any hope of mediation had faded. John Conway agrees, stating that after 1940, hopes of mediation had failed, and Pius was determined that neither side should use the

8. "The Papacy and World War II," *Journal of Ecclesiastical History* 18, no. 1 (April 1967): 72.

9. Blet, *Pie XII*, 319.

10. *Catholic Church*, 61.

11. "History and Rolf Hochhuth's *The Deputy*," in *From an Ancient to a Modern Theatre*, ed. R. G. Collins (Winnepeg: University of Manitoba Press, 1972), 151.

papacy as an ally: "Most particularly, the silence of the Papacy when apprised of the vast atrocities of the war-mongers was a deliberate policy aimed at preserving future opportunities for reconciliation, and at forestalling the kind of spiritual compromises which had so damaged the churches' reputations during the First World War."[12]

12. "Records and Documents of the Holy See," 335.

Chapter 11

A Papal Protest Would Have
Made Things Worse

The most defensible reason for Pope Pius' behavior is the best documented: that is, that he believed that a strong, direct protest against Nazi terrorism would simply make things worse for the persecuted people.

The clearest document arguing this position is one by the Pope himself, to the College of Cardinals in his traditional patronal address on June 2, 1943, in the midst of the war, in which he said, "Every single word in Our statements addressed to the competent authorities, and every one of Our public utterances, has had to be weighed and pondered by Us with deep gravity, in the very interest of those who are suffering, so as not to render their position even more difficult and unbearable than before, be it unwittingly and unintentionally."[1] While this was his only public statement, there are numerous accounts of private and more guarded words throughout the war.

In 1940, in a meeting with the Italian Ambassador Dino Alfieri, the German occupation of Poland was brought up.

1. *The Catholic Mind* 41 (September 1943): 3.

Pius said that "atrocities [were] taking place in Poland," and that "We would like to utter words of fire against such actions and the only thing restraining Us from speaking is the fear of making the plight of the victims even worse."[2] In 1943, he wrote Bishop Konrad von Preysing of Berlin that he had imposed limitations upon his protests of the German government's actions "in order to avoid greater evils."[3] In June 1963, at the height of the controversy over *The Deputy*, Cardinal Giovanni Battista Montini, a few days before he was elected Pope Paul VI, wrote a letter to the editor of *The Tablet*, the British Catholic weekly, in which he said that if Pius had "taken a position of violent opposition to Hitler in order to save the lives of those millions of Jews slaughtered by the Nazis," he "would have been guilty of unleashing on the already tormented world still greater calamities involving innumerable innocent victims." Montini had been undersecretary of state in the Vatican during the war years and he said he knew both the Pope and "the appalling conditions of war and Nazi oppression."[4] This is a compelling first-hand account of Pius' rationale.

Paolo Dezza, the Jesuit rector of the Gregorian University in Rome, recounted that Pius had said to him in December 1942, "They deplore the fact that the Pope does not speak. But the Pope cannot speak. If he spoke, things would be worse."[5] Critics as well as defenders of the Pope accept this account as valid.

In the spring of 1942, Domenico Tardini, the Vatican subsecretary of state, responded to a letter from Adam Sapieha, the Archbishop of Cracow. Tardini's note, presumably approved by Pius, stated that

2. From Montini's notes of the meeting, 13 May 1940, *ADSS* 1:423.
3. 30 April 1943, *ADSS* 2:324.
4. *The Tablet*, 29 June 1963, 714.
5. Cited in *L'Osservatore della Domenica*, 28 June 1964, in *La Documentation Catholique* (1964), 1034.

a public condemnation [of Germany] on the part of the Holy See would be amply exploited by one of the conflicting parties for political ends. Moreover the German government would . . . do two things: it would make the persecution harsher against the Catholic Poles, and it would prevent the Holy See from having any contacts in any way with the Polish bishops and from carrying out the charitable work that it can now carry out, albeit in a less forceful fashion.[6]

Pirro Scavizzi was a military chaplain attached to the hospital train of the Sovereign Order of Malta, which went to the Eastern front with Italian troops in 1942. He was used as clandestine courier to carry messages from the Polish bishops to the Vatican. Scavizzi said that when he told Pius about the conditions in Poland, the Pope replied,

Tell everyone . . . that many times [I] have thought of hurling excommunications at Nazism, of denouncing the bestiality of the extermination of the Jews to the civilized world. Serious threats of reprisal have come to our ears, not against our person, but against our unhappy sons who are now under Nazi domination. . . . After many tears and many prayers, I came to the conclusion that a protest from me would not only not help anyone, but would arouse the most ferocious anger against the Jews and multiply acts of cruelty because they are undefended. Perhaps my solemn protest would win me some praise from the civilized world, but would bring down on the poor Jews an even more implacable persecution than the one they are already enduring.[7]

Another account, published without corroboration, states that in 1942, Pius planned to "denounce the ferocity of the Nazis" to a group of Germans visiting the Vatican. He wrote out a speech, but before delivering it, read it to one of his confidantes "in a vibrant emotional and indignant voice." But then he decided not to deliver the speech, saying, "I have the duty of simplifying things, not of complicating them." According to the unnamed

6. 18 May 1942, *ADSS* 3:569–70.
7. Falconi, 238, citing the Roman monthly *La Parrocchia*, May 1964; see also Gariboldi, *Pio XII*, 152.

confidante, "this protest, the Pope reflected, would have stultified every action to save the victims of the insane Nazi dictator."[8]

In addition to these accounts, there is that of Pius' longtime housekeeper, Sister Pascalina Lehnert, who says that the Pope wrote a strong denunciation of the killing of the Jews in 1942 but burned it because he feared that more harm than good would come from it. What convinced him to do so was the effect of Dutch Archbishop Johannes de Jong's public protest against the deportation of the Dutch Jews, which resulted in greater persecutions by the Germans, to the extent of deporting Jews who had converted to Catholicism.[9] While much of Pascalina's book is colored by her devotion to the Pope, Pius' belief that he would be doing more harm than good is vouched for by others.

This view is also corroborated by Harold Tittmann, the American chargé at the Vatican. He stated in more than one dispatch that Vatican leaders told him that the Pope had "already condemned offenses against morality in wartime and that to be specific now would only make matters worse."[10] Furthermore, Tittmann reported as early as 1942 that the Vatican has "perhaps likely . . . the belief . . . that there is little hope of checking the Nazi barbarities by any method except that of physical force coming from without."[11]

Finally, it appears that Pius was asked by some persecuted Jews to avoid an explicit condemnation because it would do more harm than good.[12] Both detractors and defenders accept the argument that Pius' fear of retribution was a factor; what

---

8. From the Italian news magazine *Vita*, as cited in *The Tablet*, 11 April 1964, 419.

9. *Ich durfte ihm dienen*, 117–18. Phayer, *Catholic Church*, 94, disagrees, claiming the argument "hollow," because "the archbishop's protest was simply an excuse the Nazis used to seize these Jewish converts prematurely."

10. 3 August 1942, *FRUS* 3:772.

11. 16 October 1942, *FRUS* 3:777–78.

12. From an unsigned editorial in *La Civiltà Cattolica* 3547 (4 April 1998), 12, but without any citation of sources for this justification.

they disagree upon is its importance. John Conway sums up the defenders' views in his review of the Vatican documents: there is, he says, no evidence to support the notion that "ecclesiastical self-preservation" was the Vatican's main motive. "Pius' silence was not the outcome of ignorance or indifference; it was a deliberate choice of far-reaching reserve, seeking to prevent any escalation of violence against those who were most at risk."[13] He furthermore says that "Pius XII's talent lay in his ability to assess, far more percipiently than most of his counterparts, or indeed of his later critics, the likely results of any of his pronouncements or interventions."[14]

Michael Phayer disagrees with the argument that Pius' fear of retribution was the primary reason for his alleged silence. He bases his contention on the fact that the Pope did not speak out against the Croatian genocide in 1941 when there was no possibility of retribution.[15]

Susan Zuccotti agrees that Pius' fears against retribution against Catholics (but not Jews) was justified: "In the last analysis, then, the pope was probably correct that some Jews involved with Catholicism [i.e., converts], as well as some Catholics, would suffer from a public protest." But she also claims that a subsidiary reason for lack of a strong protest was simply embarrassment. Because Pius did not condemn the persecutions when they began, "with each week and month that passed it became more awkward and difficult to oppose measures that should have been denounced from the outset."[16]

But the first question asked by Pius' detractors is, how could things be worse? The Germans were killing all of the Jews without any mercy. A papal protest could not have made things

13. "Records and Documents of the Holy See," 333, 336.
14. "Vatican, Germany and the Holocaust," 110.
15. *Catholic Church*, 55.
16. Zuccotti, 313, 319.

worse, but it might have made things better: it might have alerted all the Jews to the fact of German intentions from an authoritative source; it would have encouraged Christians to offer refuge and help to the Jews, and it might have encouraged other Christian leaders, especially Catholic bishops in Germany and the satellite states, to speak out.

The difficulty with this question is that it assumes that Pius knew that the Germans were going to kill *all* the Jews. It is here that the problem of the time sequence is crucial for understanding the Pope's actions. It was, of course, common knowledge that the Jews were being persecuted, herded into ghettoes, and transported to eastern Europe. By late 1941 the Pope knew that large numbers of Jews were being killed by the Germans. Did he know that the Germans intended to kill *all* the Jews? If so, when did this fact become apparent to him?

Another facet of the problem is that by mid-1943 when Pius certainly knew about the ferocity of the German terror against the Jews, he was also aware of the German terror against all people. Did Pius distinguish among the victims of the Nazi terror? The Germans did not kill all of the Poles, or Greeks, or French, or other subject people. But they might be tempted to kill more if provoked by the Pope, and it appears that Pius so believed. Furthermore there were thousands of priests—both German and Polish—in German concentration camps who might have been the victims of Nazi reprisals for a papal protest; and everywhere there were Jews who had converted to Catholicism who had, in many cases, so far been spared, and who also might have suffered.

This is a most difficult problem to unravel because we do not know what would have happened if the Pope had made a strong protest. What we do know is what the Pope himself believed, according to what he said.

As a corollary to this reason, there is another that argues that

Pius feared that the humanitarian work the Vatican was doing would suffer as the result of a protest. This humanitarian work included relief to prisoners of war, tracking of captured soldiers to provide information to their families, and other forms of assistance. Robert Graham, one of Pius' most determined defenders, says that few people, including Jews, wanted a papal statement, because they were afraid that this would impede what humanitarian work the Holy See was doing: "Appeals to world opinion, high-sounding though they may appear, would have seemed cheap and trivial gestures to those engaged in rescue work."[17] The International Red Cross decided that a public protest on its part would hamper its relief work.[18] If such an organization, whose entire effort was devoted to relief work without regard to the issues involved, avoided a public protest, so much more would the papacy profit from silence in order to provide its humanitarian work.

But again, we return to the crux of the problem of Pius and the Holocaust. The Pope was not the Red Cross, whose main task was humanitarian relief. The Pope was the moral voice of Catholicism, the Vicar of Christ. The question of Pius' responsibility looms large in these circumstances: to provide for his church, of which he was the leader, or to protest for the sake of oppressed mankind? It was a cruel choice. The calculus of saving lives came into play. Would he save more by protesting or by not protesting? The question can never be answered, because we do not know what would have happened if a strong protest had been made.

17. "How to Manufacture a Legend," 21.
18. Andre Durand, *From Sarajevo to Hiroshima: History of the International Committee of the Red Cross* (Geneva: Henry Dunant Institute, 1984), 555ff.

Chapter 12

Pope Pius' Personality

When Eugenio Pacelli was elected pope in March 1939, the universal comment in the press was that he looked just like what a pope should look like. His tall, lean body, his transparent skin, his piercing eyes, all gave him an aspect of ethereal sublimity that raised him above the body of mankind. The *New York Times* correspondent in Rome, Camille Cianfarra, quoted Henry Bourdoux on Pius: "He has the sublime greatness of a mortified, almost translucent body which seems destined to serve only as a cover for his soul."[1] His appearance was compared with that of his predecessors: Pius XI, stocky and temperamental; Benedict XV, sad and weakly; Pius X, tall and stern. Throughout his pontificate, Pius XII was seen in the Catholic press as a living saint. When a film was made of him in 1942, the title was "Angelic Shepherd" (which title was supposedly based on the apocryphal St. Malachy's prophecies).[2]

Where other popes were seen as surprise victors in the

1. *The War and the Vatican* (London: Burns, Oates, & Washbourne, 1945), 81.

2. Chadwick, *Britain and the Vatican*, 210.

conclaves that chose them, Pius XII's election was expected. Only Giovanni Battista Montini, elected as Paul VI in 1963, bettered Pius XII in press predictions of election. Pius X was Patriarch of Venice, but he was a long shot and eventually became the compromise candidate because the Austrian Emperor had used his veto power against a conclave favorite. Benedict XV had been a papal diplomat and was Archbishop of Bologna, but had only just been named a cardinal the year he was elected in 1914. Pius XI was another long shot: a long career as a librarian, a short tenure as nuncio to Poland after World War I, and less than a year as Cardinal Archbishop of Milan.

As noted earlier, Pius XII was destined for the papacy. He had all of the experience in the papal curia working as nuncio and Secretary of State: the only thing he lacked was solid pastoral experience, for his episcopal title, Archbishop of Sardes, was titular only. Pius XI had endorsed him before his death, and only the fact that no Roman, nor any Secretary of State, had been elected for two centuries stood in the way of predictions of his nomination. He was elected on the third ballot on only the second day of the conclave.

We know little about the inner Pius. He did not leave a memoir, and unlike John XXIII he did not keep a diary, as far as we know. We can put together a personality from the various memoirs and recollections of those who knew or had dealings with Pius, but there is something lacking. Pius had no intimate friends. It is much easier to get a portrait of other popes' inner personalities: the tormented and haunted Paul VI, the jovial and confident John XXIII, the temperamental Pius XI, impetuous in his likes and dislikes. But of Pius XII, what can be said?

Domenico Tardini, his subsecretary of state, and later Secretary of State under John XXIII, wrote a short appreciation of Pius shortly after the Pope's death. Pius, Tardini says, was mild and shy, not a fighter—unlike Pius XI, who relished a battle. He preferred solitude and this "disposed him to avoid rather than face the battles of life." He tried to please everyone and believed the best of everyone. When he had to write a criticism of someone, he "sugar pilled" his response so as to avoid offending.[3] Pius' longtime assistant, Jesuit Robert Leiber, agrees: Pius, he says, "avoided every word which might have offended. He would say that no good ever came of hurting people."[4] He could not turn down requests, and therefore began to limit his contacts with bishops and others who might have petitions, so that he would not have to refuse them. He tended to put off decisions and spent much time agonizing over such tasks as appointments to the college of cardinals.[5] However, Tardini says, he was capable of turning others' weaknesses to his advantage.

Tardini points out one facet of his personality that bears directly upon his alleged silence: Pius, he says, saw both sides of every argument quickly, and thus was hesitant to make up his mind.[6] Cardinal Eugene Tisserant, one of the holdouts against a unanimous vote for Pius in the 1939 conclave, believed him to be indecisive.[7] Was it this mental agility that led to his equivocations and hesitations about a protest, where a person with less perception would have made a quicker decision? As Chadwick points out about Pius' hesitations on speaking out on the Holocaust, "There may be moments . . . when wisdom is not the first quality in demand, when what a moral situation needs is an explosion and let wisdom be damned."[8] Perhaps Tardini's observation about Pius' unwillingness to offend anyone is behind the contradictions between his public and private statements. When, according to Menshausen (and presuming that Menshausen was

3. *Memories,* 74. 4. "Pius as I Knew Him," 295.
5. *Memories,* 76–77. 6. *Memories,* 52.
7. Cited in Charles-Roux, 267.
8. "Pius XII," 401. Chadwick has a good discussion of Pius' personality in *Britain and the Vatican,* 50–52.

telling the truth), he told the German chargé in January 1939 that "the widespread notion that he was opposed to totalitarian states was inaccurate," and when he told Ribbentrop in March 1940 that his protests in his 1939 Christmas message were aimed at the Soviet Union, not Germany, was this his desire not to offend?[9] Perhaps these inconsistencies appear because he was essentially a writer who could voice his opinions in writing where he could use words to say exactly what he wanted his readers to hear, and he was on less sure grounds when speaking. Perhaps this is why there are such contradictory views of Pius, especially when both detractors and supporters rely on what Pius said rather than what he did or did not do. Peter Hebblethwaite, a longtime Vatican observer, agrees that Pius was hesitant about offending diplomats, but as far as the internal workings of the Church were concerned, he was decisive and vigorous; thus he was "insecure and despotic at the same time."[10]

But the problem of Pius' personality goes deeper than these matters. It has to do with the great adulation that he inspired and that in the long run no one could live up to; and to his omniscience about everything except the one thing most important to his reputation—his silence on the Holocaust.

Pius was willing to and did give talks on everything. During his nineteen-year pontificate, especially after the war, he met groups daily, everyone from nuclear physicists to dairy farmers. And he always had something to say to each of the groups that addressed its concerns. He wrote out these brief statements, and often committed them to memory; but it always appeared as if he understood the complex technology of the groups' occupations. He doted on encyclopedias and was always grateful when

9. Freidlander, *Pius XII*, 40–41, citing telegram from Menshausen to Berlin, 1 January 1940; and *ADSS* 1:356 (Tardini's notes on the conversation with Ribbentrop, told to him by Pius, 11 March 1940).

10. Peter Hebblethwaite, *In the Vatican* (Bethesda, Md.: Adler & Adler, 1968), 31–32.

he was sent a new set to add to his collection. He distrusted footnotes and citations and insisted on checking out everything himself. He apparently believed that a person capable of reading well could become an instant expert as long as he had the text to consult. The natural result was that people expected more of him than he could deliver. Analyses of his statements show no real expertise, but such is the awe a pope commands, that his listeners thought that he was well versed in the intricacies of their professions.

Part of the problem is that Pius was a trained scholar, and he approached problems with the belief that many scholars have: that common folk read encyclicals and statements as carefully as scholars do, and that they are capable of discerning meanings that appear to be hidden. Thus, he fully expected people to immediately understand his references to "persons persecuted because of their race" as referring to the Jews being killed by the Germans.

All of this came apart after he died, especially when historians began looking at his response to the Holocaust, where they found apparent equivocation and chimerical statements wrapped in papal rhetoric. It did not help that Pius was the first pope of the new media technology age. By the time he died, television was common in the developed countries; the press and documentary newsreels were present everywhere. He was the first pope to become known as a media personality, and as such, for many people he came to be the ideal pope, a stylized living icon. As a result, he was placed on a pedestal with a reputation that no person could live up to. Pius, with his perceived air of superiority, his vast learning, his willingness to pontificate on any and all subjects, simply made the situation worse. Add to this the nature of the papacy, which is that people always expect more from a pope than he can deliver, and the downfall of an icon becomes even more shattering.

It is easy to dislike Pius. He exuded none of the warmth of

his successors, especially John XXIII and John Paul II. He lacked their common touch. There is a revealing description written in 1940 by Kees Van Hoek that captures the sycophantic adulation of his admirers: Pius "is tall, majestically so. . . . One is impressed by his stature, but one is fascinated by his countenance. . . . Of great distinction, his suavity puts every visitor immediately at ease, but even with the highest of them he creates a distance of his supreme calling." And then, Van Hoek describes an incident that is even more revealing about Pius and his admirers: "I have watched his long, sleek Packard held up by the fair in a mountain village on a summer morning; he sat rigidly erect in the deep cushions reading his breviary, and nothing of the pandemonium round him diverted his attention for a second."[11] It is difficult to imagine John XXIII or John Paul II in such a situation not getting out of the car and joining the villagers in their celebration. It is also difficult to imagine a person who finds such aloofness in Pius' nature admirable.

Contrasted with this description of an aloof visage are the descriptions of Pius' actual nature, which was shy and introverted; or perhaps these go along with the aloofness. Cardinal Augustin Bea, who was his confessor for many years, says that, without violating the secrecy of the confessional, Pius was "fundamentally a lonely man in his greatness and in his keen sense of responsibility, and in this way too, he was lonely in his personal austerity and life."[12] Pius' assistant, Lieber, agrees that Pius was a loner: "He remained in solitude throughout his life."[13]

Others talk of his goodness. British Minister Osborne has the most-quoted description: "Pius XII was the most warmly humane, kind, generous, sympathetic (and incidentally saintly)

11. *Pope Pius XII, Priest and Statesman* (New York: Philosophical Library, n.d), 60.

12. *The Unity of Christians* (New York: Herder and Herder, 1963), 207.

13. "Pius as I Knew Him," 294.

character that it has been my privilege to meet in the course of a long life."[14] G. A. Grippenberg, the Finnish Ambassador to the Holy See during the war, says that Pius had a "magnetic personality [that] radiated goodness, intelligence, and a nobility of soul that was not of this world."[15] Cianfarra is a bit less adulatory: Pius, he says "is not what one would call a popular pope in the sense that the average person is made to feel he is in the presence of a human being with impulses, emotions, passions, virtues, and defects common to all men. The depth of his mind, his habit of meditation, natural aloofness, and austerity of life have made him solitary. Endowed with an iron will, Pius XII, by the constant application of self-discipline, has achieved complete control of mind and body. Thus, at times he impresses one as being a cold and distant man whose gestures and words lack spontaneity."[16]

He was learned, had a photographic memory, was punctual, and was repelled by extremes, including self-mortification.[17] He was an avid reader of newspapers and doted on dictionaries. Lieber tells us that Pius loved the classics, particularly Cicero, played the violin well and was a good horseman and swimmer in the days before he became pope.

But he had his peculiarities as well. He believed that the pope should eat alone. His longtime maid-servant, Sister Pascalina Lehnert, is a font of information on his daily life and habits. She says that he refused invitations to dine because he had a delicate stomach, but mainly because he did not want to waste time. He used his dining time to listen to foreign language radio broadcasts in order to improve his language proficiency and to catch

---

14. Cited in Chadwick, *Britain and the Vatican*, 316.

15. "Recollections of Pius XII," *America*, 18 April 1964, 539.

16 *The War and the Vatican*, 82.

17. Barrett McGurn, *A Reporter Looks at the Vatican* (New York: Coward-McCann, 1962), 67ff.

up on the news. He had a pet canary named Gretchen, whom he allowed to perch on his shoulder as he dined. He spoke German to the servants in the papal household, most of whom were German, and this led critics to claim that he was pro-German during the war. Douglas Woodruff, the editor of the *Tablet*, says that he was a perfectionist and expected the same perfectionism from his subordinates.[18]

There were a number of false stories spread about Pius. There was the rumor that when the war started in September 1939, Pius was "sleeping on the floor that he may participate more deeply in the world's suffering"; he was also reported to be fasting. The Vatican issued a prompt denial of this rumor, noting that if the Pope were making such sacrifices, he would not make the fact public.[19] In fact, Tardini tells us that during the war, "he gave out his own food, multiplied his penances, and did not want his apartment to be heated in the severe winter," so that by the end of the war, he carried only 125 pounds on his 6 foot frame.[20] Perhaps this gave rise to Leiber's recounting the preposterous story "of a well-known journalist, that the Pope slept on an iron bedstead, at which, each morning at six o'clock, he was awakened by four German Capuchin friars carrying a cup of coffee."[21] And some stories last until today. Gary Wills in 1998 repeated the ridiculous story as fact that "Pius XII's priests were instructed to take his phone calls on their knees."[22] Wills' description of John LaFarge's visit to Pius XI in 1938 would be laughable if it were not in the introduction to a sound historical

18. "Quest of Perfection: Some Personal Impressions of Pius XII," *The Tablet*, 18 October 1958, 330–31.

19. *New York Times*, 19 September 1939, 7; 23 September 1939, 5.

20. *Memories*, 41.

21. "Pius as I Knew Him," 294.

22. "The Vatican Monarchy," *New York Review of Books*, 19 February 1998, 25.

account: "As he [LaFarge] goes toward the papal chamber, a famous countenance glides by him, all sunken eyes and cheeks—Eugenio Pacelli, the pope's secretary of state—without pausing to tell him why he has been summoned."[23] LaFarge, the only eyewitness to this meeting, says of the encounter only that he met Pacelli coming out of the elevator as he was entering it and obviously had no reason to talk to him.[24] It is a testament to the problem of Pius and the Holocaust that these canards continue to be published and probably believed decades after his death.

But the spiritual side of Pius cannot be ignored when talking about his personality. He was, after all, the Pope, and he said mass daily and prayed often. Diplomats and intimates testify to his deep spirituality. Ivone Kirkpatrick, the British Minister to the Vatican in the early 1930s says, "It does not require a long conversation with Cardinal Pacelli to realise that even in politics he believes in the efficacy of prayer and the reality of divine intervention."[25] Ernst von Weizsäcker, the German Ambassador to the Vatican in 1943, says, "I was always captivated by the incomparable charm of Pius XII's intensely spiritual personality."[26] D'Arcy Osborne, the British Minister at the Vatican, called Pius "a politician in spite of himself,"[27] an allusion to his deeply religious nature that was at war with his diplomatic training.

In the end, Pius' personality caused the challenges to his reputation. However much he may have wished for humility, he

23. From the introduction to Georges Passelecq and Bernard Suchecky, *The Hidden Encyclical of Pius XI*, trans. S. Rendell (New York: Harcourt Brace, 1997), ix. Note the use of words: "glides by"—as if Pacelli were a stealth bomber; "sunken eyes and cheeks"—a frightful visage, and then doesn't tell him why he was there, as if Pacelli didn't talk to mere mortals.

24. John LaFarge, *The Manner Is Ordinary* (New York: Harcourt, Brace, 1954), 272.

25. Cited in Rhodes, 220.

26. *Memoirs*, 286.

27. As cited in Chadwick, *Britain and the Vatican*, 40.

could not rise above the obsequious adulation that was attendant upon the persona of the pope. He was a prisoner of his equivocation, his scholarly exactness, his inability to become his own person and rise above the tradition-bound concepts of the imperial papacy. And not only was his personality a factor in his reputation, it was also one in his alleged silence. His successor, John XXIII, could and did rise above the imperial papacy, and Pius suffers by contrast. Had he been followed by a less popular figure, perhaps directly by Paul VI, then the image of Pius might not be as controversial as it is today.

Chapter 13

The Effect of a Strong Protest
Virtual History

What kind of protest could Pius have made, and what would have been the effect of a strong protest? The kinds of protest—excommunication of Hitler, interdict upon Germany, even a simple statement that killing Jews was immoral—can be explained and discussed. But the effect that any one of these would have had cannot be known with any certainty. Even an informed estimate of the effect can be no better than a guess; who, for example, could have imagined that Hitler would declare war on the United States after the Japanese attacked Pearl Harbor and America's attention was directed toward the Pacific war? There are too many imponderables, and too many opportunities for simple human error or human chance, to state with any degree of accuracy what might have happened.

This difficulty has not deterred the historians. Some have offered scenarios of what would have happened had Pius made a strong protest or taken one of the actions within his power. Hochhuth's version of virtual history is that a strong papal protest, a threat to unilaterally denounce the concordat, or even perhaps to impose an interdict, would have turned millions of German Catholics against the Nazi regime. Just the threat of such a protest, he argues, would have led the regime to stop the persecution of the innocent.[1] His argument is based largely upon the simple belief that Hitler thought that German Catholics would be disposed to obey their church rather than their state. His proof for this is that Hitler held off on persecution of the Church when the war began, because he needed a unified country behind him to pursue the war effort. Hitler, he points out, had said that after the war the concordat would be dispensed with, and hence Hochhuth infers that Hitler was afraid to do anything during the war to alienate Catholics.

Many historians reject this view. Meir Michaelis, the preeminent historian of the Italian Jews, says it is not "likely that a public protest would have saved a single Jew."[2] Guenter Lewy, who is no admirer of the German bishops, says that an excommunication of Hitler or a revocation of the concordat would have had no effect; but he argues that "a flaming protest against the massacre of the Jews, coupled with the imposition of the interdict upon all of Germany or the excommunication of all Catholics in any way involved with the apparatus of the Final Solution, would have been a far more formidable and effective weapon." However, he contends, Pius could not do this "without risking the allegiance of the German Catholics" and this might have led to a "large-scale desertion from the Church."[3] Lewy concludes that if the Pope had taken the risk of alienating German Catholics, his protest probably would have failed, and "once the inability of the Pope to move the masses of the faithful into

1. *The Deputy*, 298.
2. "The Holocaust in Italy," in *The Holocaust and History: The Known, the Unknown, the Disputed and the Reexamined*, ed. M. Berenbaum and A. J. Peck (Bloomington: Indiana University Press, 1998), 453.
3. *Catholic Church*, 303

a decisive struggle against the Nazis is accepted as a fact," then a protest would have made things worse for the *Mischlinge* (half and quarter-Jews who were not being persecuted at the time) and for Catholics.[4]

Furthermore, while Hochhuth argues that Hitler feared Catholic reaction to continued persecution of the Church and therefore suspended such action for the duration of the war, he ignores the fact that Hitler continued to seize the property of some of the religious orders with no discernable effect upon German Catholics' support of the war.

Of course, we do not know what Hitler's reaction would have been to a papal protest. There was no consistency in the German reprisals. In the case of the Dutch Catholics, their bishops' protests led directly to the deportation and killing of Jews who had converted to Catholicism. In the case of the French, when their bishops protested the deportation of the Jews there were no reprisals taken against French Catholic Jews. Nor did the French protests halt the deportations of the rest of the Jews.

We do know that Pius XI's encyclical, *Mit Brennender Sorge*, of March 1937, had little effect upon German Catholics. Pius XI had denounced the Nazi regime's persecution of the German Church, along with the philosophical basis of Nazism, and especially its racism. And yet, there was no sign that most German Catholics were less supportive of the regime.

All sorts of questions arise. Could a papal protest get by German government censorship? Pius' 1939 encyclical, *Summi Pontificatus*, with its mild sympathy for the Polish people, was allowed to be read but not to be published for distribution in Germany. Would a strong papal protest be known to the German people? Would the bishops support the Pope in the imposition of an interdict? Was Hitler so determined to kill all the Jews that

4. *Catholic Church*, 305.

a papal threat would have had no effect upon him? After all, he jeopardized his war effort by the amount of energy and the resources put into the transportation and destruction of the Jews.

Carlo Falconi, one of Pius' chief critics, argues against a papal denunciation of the concordat or the imposition of an interdict; but he says that Pius should have delivered a "strong and yet loving" denunciation of Hitler and a threat to release German Catholics "from their national obedience." He also argues that a theatrical gesture, like the Danish king's threat to wear the yellow star of David that Jews were ordered to wear, would have been a powerful gesture with great effect.[5]

Should Pius have followed the apocryphal example of Bishop Felice Roeder of Beauvais? When the Vichy French government issued an edict calling upon all Jews to register with the government, Roeder, claiming Jewish ancestry, showed up at the city hall in full vestments, preceded by an acolyte carrying a crucifix.[6] For Pius to have done likewise, or to have worn a yellow star of David, would have required a shattering break with his diplomatic training and his view of the office of the papacy. But again, what would the effect have been? Would Hitler have been moved by this? Would he have taken reprisals against German Catholics and those in the occupied countries?

Falconi also argues that Pius should have sought solidarity with other Christian religions to present a united front against German terror. Cosmo Lang, the Anglican Archbishop of Canterbury, suggested such a move, but Pius refused, citing Church doctrine regarding religions not in communion with Rome. Falconi concludes that "when Pius XII identified God with his Church alone, his illusion . . . was disastrous."[7] John Conway

5. *Silence*, 99, 100.
6. *The Tablet*, 24 October 1942, 202; but there is no independent confirmation of this incident.
7. *Silence*, 102, 105.

points out that the Pope did not want to get involved with other denominations in joint relief efforts in 1940, for the same reason.[8] Would the Nazi regime have stopped its persecution in the face of a united Christian front denouncing the destruction of the innocent?

On a more moderate level, John Morley, whose study centers on papal diplomacy, says that Pius could have given orders to the nuncios "to vigorously protest the rationale behind the racial laws as a violation of justice." This might have led to a severing of relations with some states, but it "would have made clear that the Church and its diplomatic service were concerned for all men and opposed to injustice of any kind."[9] But here, we are back to the argument that Pius did not want to sever relations with Germany in particular, because he believed that the concordat preserved the Holy See's right to protest and thereby limit the anti-Catholic activities of the Nazi regime.

An argument frequently advanced is that a strong papal protest would have served to reveal that "deportation" actually meant transportation to a death camp;[10] it would also have served as a warning to the Jewish community that the German regime was bent on their destruction and therefore the Jews would have been able to hide from their tormentors. Pius' defenders argue in response that even knowledge of the German plans would not have saved the Jews because of the power of the German machine of destruction. William D. Rubinstein claims that the Allies could do nothing to save the Jews, other than end the war earlier, so powerful were the Germans within the confines of the German *Grossraum*. Rubinstein says, "In all likelihood—a likelihood probably amounting to a near-certainty—Hitler would have paid no heed

8. "The Vatican and the Holocaust: A Reappraisal," *Miscellanea Historiae Ecclesiasticae* 9 (1984):479.

9. *Vatican Diplomacy*, 209.

10. Lewy, 303.

whatever to any pronouncement on the Jews made by the Vatican. . . . Theoretically and in hindsight, the Pope might have excommunicated all Catholic members of the SS (or of the Nazi Party) although the only likely effect of such a pronouncement would have been that the Nazis denounced the Pope as an agent of 'Judeo-Bolshevism' and an imposter."[11] Furthermore, the Jews knew what the Germans were doing, from reports of their own leaders and those who escaped from the death camps.

It is thus impossible to tell what the effect of a papal protest would have been. The possibilities and the risks that have been outlined are precisely the ones that Pius had to consider. The record appears to show that Pius had no base motives for his alleged silence and, in fact, had the noble motive of protecting innocent lives by not making a strong protest. A different pope might have done otherwise, might have made a strong protest, and the result might have been catastrophic, as Pope Paul VI said in his commentary on Hochhuth's drama. If so, it would have preserved and enhanced the moral integrity of the papacy; at what cost it is impossible to tell. Perhaps Pius, in grappling with the cruel choice, foresaw this outcome and decided that a forceful protest would cause more harm than good, even though he knew that his reputation might suffer.

11. *The Myth of Rescue* (New York: Routledge, 1997), 101. See the dispute over Rubinstein's claim in the *Times Literary Supplement,* 10 October 1997, 9–10; and 7 November 1997, 19.

Chapter 14

Pius and the Countries of German-Dominated Europe

It is a common fallacy to believe that the pope—any pope—has absolute control over Catholic clergy throughout the world. In the Europe of World War II, there were more than 600 bishops and 250,000 priests. Many of the bishops had not been chosen freely by the Vatican; in most cases, concordats had been concluded that gave the civil power some control over episcopal appointments. In all cases, the papal nuncios had great influence in selecting bishops. Pius knew only a few bishops well, probably the German ones better than others, for he had helped select some of them in the 1920s when he served as nuncio to Germany.

A pope has even less control over individual priests. They are the products of seminaries regulated by bishops, who in large dioceses may have only a slight knowledge of their priests. Regular clergy—those in religious orders—are generally better known to their abbots or superiors and are under greater control of ecclesiastical discipline, but unless they are prominent theologians or have some other public role, they are unknown to a pope.

In any case, control by a pope is more apparent than real. Furthermore, papal knowledge of an individual priest's or bishop's activities is happenstance. Nor is there any way that a pope can be certain that his orders will be carried out. In many cases they can be comfortably and subtly ignored. As a result, popes seldom give orders to priests. Disciplinary action is based on infractions of existing canon law, and usually through the bishop, because otherwise a pope would be unlikely to know.

Therefore, in the circumstances of World War II, whether an individual bishop or priest helped persecuted Jews, or helped the persecutors, or did nothing, was usually beyond the control of the Pope. If he made demands, or if he simply requested that his orders be followed, it was up to the individual priest or bishop to comply. In some countries, the Pope asked that the convents and other religious institutions be opened to offer refuge to the persecuted. In others, the nuncio did likewise, usually with the consent or urging of the Pope. On this point, and despite his sharp criticism of Pius for not speaking out against the Holocaust as an encouragement to bishops, Michael Phayer says, "It would be a mistake to imagine that Pope Pius was in a position to dictate church policy regarding the persecution of the Jews to the bishops of a country."[1]

The nuncios carried out the policy of the Holy See. We can assume that Pius, as a trained diplomat, was in direct control of the Secretariat of State and the nuncios. There is little question that he was a competent administrator and that the Curia was under his control as well. In any event, the Secretary of State and the nuncios were appointed by the Pope and therefore he was responsible for what they did. Presumably if they did something he did not like they would be admonished, or even recalled. However, it appears that Pius had to take other factors

1. *Catholic Church*, 83.

into consideration when faced with a nuncio of whom he disapproved. (This seems most apparent in the case of Berlin nuncio Cesare Orsenigo's usual craven attitude toward the German regime to which he was accredited; Pius was apparently hesitant to remove him for fear that the Nazi government would not allow a replacement, and a weak nuncio was better than none at all to protect the rights of the Church.)[2] Thus, lacking evidence otherwise, in dealing with all of these countries the assumption will be made that the nuncios and the Secretary of State spoke and acted for the Pope, keeping in mind the vagaries of time and distance and the need for nuncios to respond quickly to events without waiting for a message to go to Rome and back.

These facts must be kept in mind in relating the story of Pius XII and the Holocaust. Where the Pope acted to protect Jews, and where he did not seize the opportunity to do so—these are the specific instances to be examined here. As for the action or inaction of other clerics, those stories belong to the larger topic of the Church and the Holocaust. Herein we are concerned only with Pope Pius XII.

One of the statistics often cited by Pius' defenders is the statement by Pinchas Lapide, an Israeli diplomat. Lapide says, "The Catholic Church, under the pontificate of Pius XII was instrumental in saving at least 700,000, but probably as many as 860,000 Jews from certain death at Nazi hands." The way Lapide arrived at this figure is by stating that there were 1,300,000 European Jews who survived the Holocaust; he then "deducted all reasonable claims of rescue made by the Protestant Churches . . . as well as those saved by Communists, self-declared ag-

2. Chadwick, *Britain and the Vatican*, 21ff.; Falconi, 139. Supposedly Orsenigo's behavior so angered the Pope that he did not create him a cardinal, as was traditional, when he was recalled from Germany after the war. See the favorable biography by Monica M. Biffi, *Mons. Cesare Orsenigo: Nunzio Apostolico in Germania (1930–1946)* (Milan: NED, 1997).

nostics and other non-Christian Gentiles." The result is "at least 700,000, but in all probability is much closer to the maximum of 860,000."[3] Lapide gives no documentation for this figure nor his exact calculations. It should be noted that Lapide does not say that Pius saved the Jews, only that the saving occurred "under the pontificate of Pius XII." The undocumented calculation and suggestive wording have been ignored by Pius' defenders. Their uncritical acceptance of Lapide's statistics and statements has weakened their arguments.

Many Jewish groups now argue that the Jewish praise for Pius in 1945 was the result of relief at the end of the war, and the lack of knowledge that they had of Pius' alleged silence. Historian Susan Zuccotti supports them, claiming that such expressions of gratitude were "rooted in benevolent ignorance." She further argues that the praise originated with foreigners in Italy and that the Jews went along with the praise so as to prevent a recrudescence of anti-Semitism; she also argues that some wanted the Pope to look favorably upon their attempts to recover Jewish children from the Catholic institutions they had been placed in for safekeeping during the war.[4]

Neither extreme defenders nor extreme critics have so far been willing to temper their views with acceptance of the facts. Hence the purpose of this section: to attempt an understanding of papal actions in German-dominated Europe.

Italy

Pius XII was an Italian, a Roman, and above all, the Bishop of Rome and Primate of all Italy. Italian events were therefore more important to him than anything else. He also had more power in Italy than anywhere else, chiefly because by the time

---

3. *Three Popes and the Jews* (New York: Hawthorn Books, 1967), 214–15.
4. Zuccotti, 301–3.

he was elected Pope, Mussolini's regime had become a disappointment to most Italians. Mussolini had led them into an alliance with Hitler that they did not like, and in 1940 he led them into a war that few supported. It was natural in such a situation that many Italians would turn to the Pope as the one person who could represent them.[5]

The Italian entry into the war placed Pius in a precarious position. The Lateran Accords, signed in 1929, stipulated that the Holy See not get involved in Italian politics. This was interpreted to mean that it must remain neutral in any conflict involving Italy. As the war continued and the Italians lost their African conquests, the Germans began using Italy as a conduit to reinforce and supply the Afrika Korps. Pius' position became even more precarious. It worsened in September 1943 when the Allies invaded Italy and Italy surrendered, whereupon the Germans occupied most of Italy. Rome came under German military occupation. There was no effective Italian government; even the Fascists were under German rule. As a result, the Pope, who was not under German control, became a beacon of hope and independence to the Italians. But Pius felt exposed. The Germans could arrest and harm him at any time. He was aware that Hitler had talked about a plan to kidnap him, and in any event, with the vagaries of war, anything was possible.[6] More than ever it was necessary for him to move cautiously; although he was not concerned for his personal safety, he feared for the governance of the Church should he be abducted.

The first event in his relationship with Italian Jews was a ran-

5. See Italo Garzia, "Pope Pius XII, Italy and the Second World War," in *Papal Diplomacy in the Modern Age*, ed. P. Kent and J. F. Pollard, 121–36, and his larger work, *Pio XII e l'Italia nella seconda guerra mondiale* (Brescia: Morcelliana, 1988). Zuccotti, highly critical of the Pope, describes and analyzes the situation in Italy.

6. Owen Chadwick, "Weizsäcker, the Vatican, and the Jews of Rome," *Journal of Ecclesiastical History* 28, no. 2 (April 1977): 183.

som demand from the Germans in late September 1943: the Jewish community in Rome must turn over 50 kilos of gold within thirty-six hours. When it appeared that the Jewish leaders could not come up with the necessary amount, they approached the Vatican, through intermediaries, and Pius offered a loan to make up the difference; he stipulated that there would be no interest on the loan and there was no time limit set for paying back the amount.

This matter has been misinterpreted by some authors, with statements that the Pope melted down sacred vessels to make up the amount.[7] The United Press carried a dispatch that was printed in the *New York Times* on October 17, 1943, stating that the Pope had "contributed a considerable amount" to the ransom. In fact, enough contributions came in from Jews and Christians that the papal loan was not needed. No one now disputes these facts. But it is argued that as a result, when word spread through the Jewish community of the offer, it confirmed the Jews in the notion that the Pope would be their protector against the Germans and therefore they were less likely to be concerned about rumors that the Germans intended to arrest and transport them.[8] Furthermore, the Jews of Rome, despite centuries of Christian persecution, had always looked to the popes as protectors against Catholic anti-Semitism.

Less than a month later, the Germans rounded up as many of the Roman Jews as they could find and transported them to Auschwitz, where they were killed. This action raises the question of the Pope's role in the event. It is the subject of great controversy, probably the most intense of the entire question of Pius and the Holocaust. It is the central fact in Hochhuth's drama.

7. See, for example, Oscar Halecki, *Pius XII—Pope of Peace* (New York: Creative Age Press, 1951), 192.

8. Zuccotti, 150–70, analyzes the ransom demand and the October roundup in detail.

The first dispute about the October roundup is over Pius' foreknowledge of the event. Most writers agree that when the roundup plans were sent to the German authorities in Italy some weeks before it occurred, Pius was most certainly informed through various sources. Susan Zuccotti argues that he had the opportunity and the obligation to inform the Jews and thus give them time to escape.[9] However, Chadwick makes the implied argument that the Pope did not believe that the Germans would actually carry out their plans, especially after the Jews had paid the ransom gold. He says that Pius was visibly upset at the news of the roundup; the implication is that Pius did not know when or indeed *if* the roundup would take place.[10]

Another, more important, point of controversy has to do with the interpretation of the reports to Berlin of Ernst von Weizsäcker, the German Ambassador to the Vatican.[11] Weizsäcker was a career diplomat who had little use for the Nazis. He had been permanent undersecretary of state in Berlin until the summer of 1943, just before the Italian surrender, when he was named Ambassador to the Holy See. He was opposed to any action against the Roman Jews, because he believed that it would prompt the Pope to protest and therefore would ruin the papal policy of neutrality and turn the world against Germany. Whether he sincerely believed that the persecution of the Jews was inhumane is another question, and beside the point here, because he wanted to prevent a roundup in any event.

Weizsäcker encouraged the Pope to be silent about this atroc-

9. Zuccotti, 158.

10. "Weizsäcker, the Vatican and the Jews of Rome," 190.

11. Chadwick, "Weizsacker, the Vatican and the Jews of Rome," basing his account on the article by Weizsäcker's biographer, Leonidas Hill, "The Vatican Embassy of Ernst von Weizsäcker, 1943–1945," *Journal of Modern History* 39 (1967): 138–59, which has the best insight into the German Ambassador's actions.

ity. A papal protest, he feared, would not only destroy the Vatican's neutrality and thereby prevent any possibility of a papal mediation of the war; it might also anger Hitler to the point that he would kidnap the Pope. Either would have disastrous effects upon Germany's policies; and when Weizsäcker was called in by Cardinal Maglione, the Secretary of State, who asked the Ambassador to intervene to free the arrested Jews, Weizsacker told Maglione that "any protest by the pope would only result in the deportations being carried out more vigorously."[12] Then Weizsäcker wrote to Berlin in support of a letter that Bishop Alois Hudal, the rector of the German College in Rome, had written to the SS commander in Rome. Hudal had asked, in the name of the Pope (but apparently without papal knowledge), for a suspension of the arrests; otherwise there might be a public papal protest. The arrests were stopped, but the first train had already left Rome bound for Auschwitz. Michaelis claims that the Germans stopped the arrests not because of the threat of a papal protest, but because they had run their course.[13]

Weizsäcker's letter to Berlin contained the fateful phrase that was used by Hochhuth and every other critic: he said the arrests "took place, in a manner of speaking, under the Pope's own windows."[14] In fact, the roundup in the Roman Jewish ghetto was over a mile away from the Pope's Vatican apartments, but sufficiently close to validate Weizsäcker's comment.

Then, a few days later, Weizsäcker wrote to Berlin again that Pius had not made a statement of protest because he did not want to "strain relations with the German Government" and that an article in *L'Osservatore Romano* (25–26 October 1943) which stated that the Pope was solicitous of the wartime persecuted,

12. Chadwick, "Weizsäcker, the Vatican and the Jews of Rome," 191.
13. Michaelis, 369.
14. Cited in Chadwick, "Weizsäcker, the Vatican and the Jews of Rome," 194.

including all persons regardless of race, was so convoluted with papal rhetoric that "only very few people will recognize in it a special allusion to the Jewish question."[15] Pius' critics have cited this statement as proof of the Pope's pro-German sentiments. Friedlander says that when Weizsäcker "reported particularly welcome information on the attitude of the Sovereign Pontiff, of the Curia or of the nuncio in Berlin toward the Reich, the information tended to be accurate."[16]

Chadwick, however, says that Weizsäcker purposely downplayed the article in *L'Osservatore Romano* to calm Berlin's fears that the article was in fact anti-German, so as to prevent any hostile action against the Pope and also to prevent further roundups that might push Pius to make a public protest. He claims that Weizäcker's statements, which have been used to damn the Pope, were done purposely in order to convince the German government that further action against the Jews would prompt a papal protest. Chadwick concludes that "Weizsäcker has been blamed for twisting his reports and, for the sake of immediate protection of Rome and the pope, destroying the pope's reputation with posterity. But it is arguable that a man doing the best that he can for human beings in terrible circumstances can hardly be wrong to let men's posthumous reputations take care of themselves."[17] Conway points out that the threat of a protest thus had the effect of a protest itself.[18] Alvarez and Graham say that Weiszäcker maneuvered his move from permanent state secretary in the German Foreign Office to the Vatican Embassy because he believed that Germany was losing the war by 1943 and he wanted to use his influence to get Hitler to accept papal mediation. But he believed that the only way that Hitler would accept such

15. Michaelis, 371, citing the document.
16. *Pius XII*, xxi–xxii.
17. "Weizsäcker, the Vatican and the Jews of Rome," 196–97.
18. "The Vatican, Germany, and the Holocaust," 115.

mediation was to be convinced that the Pope was sympathetic to Germany. Hence, he sent messages back to Berlin to that effect.[19]

The Vatican documents do not put the Pope in a favorable light in this matter. According to Maglione's minutes of his conversation with Weizsäcker, the Secretary of State had called in the Ambassador to protest the roundup, and when Weizsäcker asked what the Pope would do if the roundups continued, Maglione said that the "Holy See would not want to be in the position of having to say words of disapproval," and later that the Holy See is "cautious so as not to give the German people the impression that it has done or has wished to do even the slightest thing against Germany during this terrible war."[20] These excerpts have been variously interpreted; critics take them at face value, while defenders of the Pope argue that they must be seen in the wider context of the entire papal policy of maintaining impartiality in order to mediate the war.

In her striking criticism of the Pope's behavior during the roundup, Zuccotti says, "It is at least arguable, then, that Pius XII cannot be faulted for delivering no public condemnation of the October roundup during the less than forty-eight hours when the arrested Jews were still detained. . . . But he should have informed the Germans privately, long before October 16, that he would take a public stand against any Jewish deportations." And the Pope "should have issued an immediate and loud protest" once the train carrying the Jews out of Rome left the station. This would have alerted Jews everywhere as to the Germans' intentions.[21] Zuccotti claims that one of the reasons for papal silence in Italy was that the Pope was "in an awkward position" because he had not protested German persecution of the Jews in

19. *Nothing Sacred,* 7–8.
20. 16 October 1943, *ADSS* 9:505–6.
21. Zuccotti, 165–66.

other countries, and "a protest in October 1943 would draw attention to those earlier silences."[22] Even if this rationale is accepted as valid, it appears to be one of the less important reasons for the Pope's alleged silence.

About the same time, in late October 1943, an agreement was reached between the Germans and the Holy See whereby the Vatican and its buildings outside the Vatican proper were granted neutral status, and therefore protection from German intrusion. Almost 5,000 Roman Jews took advantage of this situation to seek shelter in the Vatican and its buildings and in the convents and monasteries of Rome. Countless others were saved in the convents and monasteries of all of Italy.[23]

There is evidence that Pius intervened to protect Jews in German-occupied northern Italy after Rome was liberated by American and British armies in early June 1944. He asked Weizsäcker to prevent further deportations, but the German government did not respond to his appeal.[24]

There is criticism of the Pope's unwillingness to publicly protest other German persecutions in Italy. These include the Ardeatine Cave massacre, in which 335 Italian hostages, including a few Jews, were killed in reprisal for an attack on the German garrison in Rome.[25] There is also criticism of Pius' requesting that the Germans maintain order in Rome against violence as a reaction to the roundup of October 16 and later persecutions; presumably he feared the violence might lead not only to a left-wing anticlerical government being established if the Germans

22. Zuccotti, 167–68
23. Michaelis, 365.
24. Michaelis, 395–96.
25. Robert Katz, *Black Sabbath* (New York: Macmillan, 1969); Katz' book is a powerful narrative based on extensive interviews with survivors and killers alike, but apparently without a direct reading of the Vatican documents that had already been published by that time; he relied on *The New York Times* articles based on their publication.

were forced out, but also to the destruction of the monuments and artistic treasures of Rome.[26]

The complex of relationships between the Pope and the Italian bishops is difficult to untangle. Was the behavior of the bishops—either helping Jews or failing to help (in the case of one or two bishops)—the result of orders from the Pope? Were there specific orders? There is some evidence that Pius sent secret orders to the Italian bishops to help the Jews. Robert Graham cites the case of Assisi, where the bishop opened the doors of his religious institutions to the Jews in September 1943. The bishop showed one of his priests a letter from the Vatican Secretary of State asking for aid to the persecuted and said, "This is the will of the Holy Father Pius XII. It has to be done with the maximum of secrecy and prudence. No one even among the priests should know about it."[27] Supporters of the Pope use such examples as evidence that there was a specific papal order; detractors claim that what aid was given was done so in spite of papal silence. Zuccotti, in particular, devotes much of her study to denying that the Pope ordered the Italian clergy to help the Jews; she claims that the story that the Pope sent large amounts of aid to the convents and monasteries harboring Jewish refugees is simply a myth. At the same time she says a papal order was not technically necessary, for religious houses could admit guests without papal authorization; it certainly would have helped, however, because many Jews were either refused shelter or obtained it only

26. Katz, 258–59. Phayer, *Catholic Church*, 104, says that Pius freely criticized the Germans after they were forced out of Rome but not during the occupation, because he feared that they might destroy the Eternal City.

27. Cited in Robert Graham, "Relations of Pius XII and the Catholic Community with Jewish Organizations," in *The Italian Refuge: The Rescue of Jews during the Holocaust*, ed. Ivo Herzer (Washington: The Catholic University of America Press, 1989), 250. Zuccotti, 263–64 doubts the existence of such a letter, but offers no proof other than conjecture.

with great difficulty.[28] It does seem, though, that despite the absence of written documentation, such a large-scale rescue could not have been attempted without implied papal approval, and certainly Pius must have approved the use of Vatican buildings, including his summer residence at Castelgandolfo, for the protection of the Jews.

France

Two major issues are raised by critics concerning Pius in his dealings with the situation in France. These are the Bérard report and the Pope's failure to criticize personally the German persecution of the French Jews. There is also the lesser issue of Cardinal Eugène Tisserant's appeal to Pius for a strong statement of protest.

After the French surrender in June 1940, France was divided in two: northern France, under the direct control of the Germans, and Vichy France, with a semi-independent regime under Philippe Pétain. With the division, the nuncio, Valerio Valeri, moved south from Paris and remained accredited to the Vichy regime.

Much of the anti-Semitism of the Vichy regime was directed against foreign rather than French Jews, namely German Jews who had fled Germany when the persecutions began there in the 1930s, and Belgian and Dutch Jews who had fled the invasion in May 1940. These foreign Jews were singled out as creating a

28. Zuccotti, 194–95. Throughout her work she details instances of aid claimed and refutes most of them. It does appear, however, that she does not give the Pope the benefit of the doubt. For example, she says that the nuns at a convent harboring Jews regularly received foodstuffs from the Vatican, "but there is no way to know how much food was delivered. There is also no reason to believe that any supplies were intended specifically for Jews" (194). Her book is replete with statements of this sort.

problem for the Vichy regime and for France in general. Even before the Germans demanded it, the Vichy regime decreed anti-Semitic legislation in the fall of 1940, and it followed these laws with further legislation depriving Jews of civil rights.[29] In August 1941, Pétain asked his ambassador to the Vatican if the Holy See had any objections to the anti-Semitic legislation. Léon Bérard, the Ambassador, sent a reply on September 2, 1941, which stated that "in principle, there is nothing in these measures which the Holy See would find to criticize," and that "I have been told by an authorized person at the Vatican [that] no quarrel will be started with us over the statute for the Jews." Bérard said, however, that the Vatican representatives asked "that in the application of the law, the precepts of justice and charity be taken into account." While the substance of Bérard's report stated that the Church made no distinctions about race, and further, that the Church had the right to make rules about marriage (and therefore a Catholic could marry a Jew if the Church approved, in opposition to the racial legislation), still, he claimed, the Church authorities said it was legitimate to "limit [Jewish] activity in society and . . . to restrict their influence."[30]

When Pétain brought this matter up with the nuncio, Valeri said that the report was based on false information. When Valeri informed Cardinal Maglione, the Secretary of State noted that Bérard had told him that his sources for his report were Tardini and Montini.[31] A month later, Maglione, in a letter to Valeri, said that Pétain was making "exaggerated deductions" from the Bérard report (in assuming that the Vatican had no objections to the anti-Semitic law), and further, that the law was "unfortunate."[32]

Friedlander admits that Bérard's report "must be read with

29. Michael R. Marrus and Robert O. Paxton, *Vichy France and the Jews* (New York: Basic Books, 1981), 3ff.
30. Cited in Friedlander, *Pius XII*, 95, 97, 98–99.
31. 30 September 1941, *ADSS* 8:295–97.
32. 31 October 1941, *ADSS* 8:333–34.

great caution and says it "seems difficult to prove." Yet, he argues that the report provides "a significant insight into the attitude of the Holy See concerning the discriminatory legislation."[33] Thus, Friedlander has it both ways: he admits that the report is suspect as reflecting the views of the Vatican, but at the same time it does reflect the views of the Vatican.

Victor Conzemius asks the simple question of Friedlander, namely, which document appears more trustworthy as reflecting the views of the Vatican: that of an unnamed "Vatican official" filtered through the views of the French ambassador, or the clear statement of the Secretary of State?[34] And, Henri de Lubac, in his memoirs, says that the Bérard report makes no sense as claimed to have been based on official Vatican views and strongly hints that the Ambassador made up the report on his own.[35]

Was Pius silent on other matters of the persecution of French Jews? There are reports that the Pope told various bishops to protest the persecutions, but there is no written record of such insructions.[36] On the other hand, there are records of protests by nuncio Valeri to Pétain and other authorities. Given the number of these protests, it must be assumed that Valeri had cleared his protests with the Pope, or even had protested at the urging of Pius.[37] *L'Osservatore Romano* published protests, and Vatican Radio broadcast protests.[38]

In his survey, historian W. D. Halls says, "There appears to be no evidence that the Pope or the Vatican gave any practical sup-

33. *Pius XII*, 99.

34. *Eglises chretiennes et totalitarisme national-socialiste: un bilan historiographique* (Louvain: Publications universitaires de Louvaiu, 1969), 61.

35. *Christian Resistance to Anti-Semitism: Memories from 1940–1944*, trans. Sister Elizabeth Englund (San Francisco: Ignatius Press, 1990), 82ff.

36. W. D. Halls, *Politics, Society and Christianity in Vichy France* (Oxford: Berg, 1995), 139.

37. Morley, 54ff. documents some of these protests, while at the same time discounting them as ineffective.

38. Halls, 127–28.

port to the saving of French Jews. . . . This inertia is all the more surprising, because elsewhere in occupied Europe papal intervention was vigorous and effective."[39] It may be that the Pope intervened where the bishops did not, for the French bishops were most active in denouncing the persecutions. In his letter to German Bishop Konrad von Preysing, Pius said that he was leaving it up to individual bishops to protest because they knew the local situation better than he did.[40] Whether his own protest would have added weight is at the heart of the entire controversy of Pius and the Holocaust.

Finally, there is the matter of the Tisserant letter. In June 1940, as France was on the verge of surrendering to Germany, Cardinal Eugène Tisserant, a member of the papal Curia in Rome, wrote a letter to Cardinal Emmanuel Suhard, the Archbishop of Paris. Tisserant told Suhard, "I have asked the Holy Father with insistence, since the beginning of December [1939], to issue an encyclical on the duty of the individual to obey the dictates of his conscience, because this is a vital point of Christianity. . . . I fear that history will reproach the Holy See for having followed a policy of comfort and convenience, and not much else."[41]

Tisserant said, when the letter was published in 1964 at the height of the controversy over *The Deputy*, that he had no intention of criticizing the Pope, but rather his colleagues in the Curia: "In a letter to Cardinal Suhard, I was a bit violent, but what I had in mind was something [not] applicable only to Nazism or Marxism or Fascism, but something that might apply to everyone who follows orders blindly without listening to his own conscience." At the same time, he admitted that Pius had done exactly what he had asked for: "It seems evident to me that [the] principles, reaffirmed by Pope Pacelli in his first encyclical

39. Halls, 128.
40. 30 April 1943, *ADSS* 2:318–27.
41. Cited in *The Tablet*, 4 April 1964, 389.

and repeated forcefully in every circumstance, above all in the Christmas messages of the war years, constitute the most concrete condemnation of the Hitlerian type of absolutism."[42] Tisserant added that Pius had planned a public protest against "the tragedy into which Hitler plunged innocent victims, first of all the Jews," but that the Pope "chose underground action on behalf of the Jews in preference to protests; he did this solely to avoid aggravating their tragic situation."[43]

It is difficult to reconcile these 1964 statements with his wartime request for an encyclical. A year later, in 1965. he appeared to reverse himself again. In a letter to Saul Friedlander, upon receipt of the author's *Pius XII and the Third Reich*, a work critical of Pius, Tisserant said, "I admired the wealth of your documentation. . . . It is well that the whole truth be known. It was very difficult during the war to know exactly what was going on."[44]

Poland

Unlike the cases of Italy and France, there is little dispute among historians over the facts of Pius' relations with the Poles. His contacts with the Polish bishops and occasionally the laity are contained in two volumes of the Vatican documents. Where historians differ is in their interpretations. Pius' detractors emphasize the many requests from Poles, both clergy and laity, for a protest against the Germans, while his defenders emphasize the Pope's rationale for not speaking out forcefully.

42. Cited in *New York Times*, 26 February 1964, 41.

43. Cited in *The Tablet*, 11 April 1964, 418–419.

44. The letter is dated March 4, 1965, and is published in the frontispiece of Friedlander's book. Close reading of the letter can lead to different interpretations, one being that Tisserant does not endorse Friedlander's conclusions, but that he is glad to see the documentation published.

Even before the war began, Pius was criticized for urging the Poles to give in to Hitler's demands in order to prevent the conflict. Did this indicate a special concern for the Germans and an indifference to Polish interests? It appears more likely that Pius wanted to prevent war by attempting to solve what most diplomats saw as one of the most contentious feature of the Versailles Treaty, namely the question of the Polish Corridor. The German demands of the summer of 1939 were for the territory they had lost in 1919 and did not include all of the Polish territory that was taken after the war broke out. The Pope, along with many Western diplomats, could not know that Hitler was intent upon dominating all of Poland.

When Poland was overrun and divided by the Germans and Soviets in September 1939, Pope Pius was faced with a number of problems. The most important was to find some means to provide for the spiritual needs of the Polish people. This was a greater problem in German-occupied Poland, because most of the people in that area were Catholics, while the majority in the Soviet zone were Jews and Orthodox, although there were some Uniate Christians in communion with Rome. The Germans arrested a large number of Polish clergy, including bishops, and placed numerous restrictions upon their religious practices. Furthermore, they refused to allow the nuncio to Germany to visit their zone, arguing that the 1933 concordat with Germany did not apply to conquered areas. And, in June 1940, the Germans ordered that Polish clergy could not leave Poland. This meant that there was no secure means of communication with Polish clergy. Pius had to use chaplains in the Italian army involved in the invasion of the Soviet Union after June 1941 to communicate with the Poles.

Undoubtedly the Polish problem concerned Pius more than any other at the time; it was compounded by the numerous requests from Polish clergy and laity (along with French diplomats) to condemn the German invasion and to protest the atrocities that were happening daily in Poland. The Pope felt that quiet diplomacy was the best way to resolve both problems.[45] His response was not satisfying to the Poles. He spoke to the Polish colony in Rome on September 30, 1939, with words of sympathy but not of protest.[46] To complaints that he was indifferent, *L'Osservatore Romano* responded that "feeling and expressions which may be allowed—and sometimes only tolerated—on the part of the faithful and the members of the local hierarchy of one of the belligerent countries, would not be desirable, much less expected, on the part of the visible head of the Church."[47]

He offered sympathy, but again no protest, in his encyclical *Summi Pontificatus* in October. Three months later, Vatican Radio, under Pius' specific direction, denounced German persecution, comparing it to that of the Spanish anticlericals in 1936 and saying that "the Germans use the same methods as the Soviets—perhaps even worse ones."[48] Then, after complaints from the Nazi regime,[49] Pius ordered a halt to such broadcasts because, as he later told German Bishop von Preysing, he did "not want to impose useless sacrifices on German Catholics" who were facing reprisals from the Nazi regime.[50] This action compounded Polish frustration.

Angering the Poles even more—both those in Poland and those in the government in exile in London—were reports man-

---

45. On the topic of the Pope and Poland, there is an excellent brief account in Conzemius, "Le Saint-Siège," 468–72. Phayer, *Catholic Church*, 20–30, is one of the most critical of Pius. The most satisfying study is Alessandro Duce, *Pio XII e la Polonia (1939–1945)* (Rome: Edizione Studium, 1997), which is solidly based on archival research.

46. *ADSS* 3:84.

47. 15 October 1939, in *ADSS* 3:96–99.

48. Cited in Blet, *Pie XII*, 89–90.

49. Notes of Montini, 27 January 27 1940, *ADSS* 3:208–209.

50. 22 April 1940, *ADSS* 2:140–41.

ufactured by the Germans that the Pope was on the side of the Axis powers. He was depicted as an Italian first and a cleric second. The Polish primate, Cardinal Augustus Hlond, from his exile in France, sent these complaints to the Pope.[51] Archbishop Adam Sapieha of Cracow also wrote, asking for a papal protest, saying that while such a protest might have no effect upon the Germans, it would give moral aid to the Poles and would defend the principles of justice.[52] Maglione, the Secretary of State, responded to all of these complaints pointing out that the Pope had not been silent, that papal expressions of sympathy for the Poles were sufficient, and that the Pope preferred to work through diplomatic channels to put an end to the suffering.[53] Sapieha came around to understanding the Pope's position;[54] in particular, after he received a letter from the Pope addressed to the Polish bishops he told the Pope that he was afraid to publicize it for fear of greater "victimization" of his clergy and laity.[55] However, reflecting the Cracow archbishop's ambivalent attitude toward a papal protest, a few months later he asked for a new papal letter containing the substance of the earlier ones, but requested that it be published in the official *Acta Apostolicae Sedis* instead of being sent to the bishops; in this way the Pope's message would get out without exposing the Polish bishops to German suspicions.[56] Such a letter was drafted, but was never sent; it spoke only in very general terms about the persecution, but with no mention of the Germans.[57] Instead, Pius alluded to the persecution in his patronal address of June 2, 1943, but there was

51. 2 August 1941, *ADSS* 3:418–22.
52. 3 November 1941, *ADSS* 3:489–91.
53. 3 September 1941, *ADSS* 3:450–52.
54. 2 February 1942, *ADSS* 3:528–29.
55. 28 October 1942, *ADSS* 3:669–70.
56. 23 March 1943, *ADSS* 3:769–70.
57. 31 May 1943, *ADSS* 3:798–801.

no express condemnation of the Germans. Sapieha appeared pleased with this.[58]

But the strongest complaint against the Pope came from Karol Radonski, Bishop of Wloclawek, who was in exile in London and in contact with the Polish government in exile. He wrote to Rome complaining that the faithful in Poland were being "increasingly alienated" from the Pope. All sorts of terrible things were happening, he said, "and the Pope is silent, as if he cared nothing for his flock." Furthermore, he said that the Germans were claiming that their activities in Poland were done with papal consent, and when the Pope did not deny this, the Polish people believed it to be true.[59] When Maglione chastised him for "adding an additional cross" for the Pope to carry, and said that the Pope would follow his own conscience on what to do,[60] Radonski replied that he had heard that the nuncio in France (Valeri) had told Pétain that the Pope had condemned the persecution of Jews. "Are we less deserving than the Jews?" he asked. Moreover, the Vatican's excuse, that papal silence was in order to prevent further persecution, was not working. "When such crimes cry to heaven for vengeance, the inexplicable silence of the highest teacher in the Church is an occasion of spiritual ruin to those—and their number is legion—who do not know the reason."[61]

This appeal had no effect upon the Pope. In numerous messages, Maglione restated the Pope's position that the Pope must remain neutral in order to be effective, and that the Polish bishops themselves recognized that the persecution that would be intensified by a papal protest.[62] Undersecretary Tardini had already

58. 18 June 1943, *ADSS* 3:813–14.
59. 14 September 1942, *ADSS* 3:633–36.
60. 9 January 1943, *ADSS* 3:713–17.
61. 15 February 1943, *ADSS* 3:736–39.
62. 26 May 1942, *ADSS* 3:574–84, is one of the clearest.

given the classic papal position on all papal protests: he said a papal protest would be

amply exploited by one of the conflicting parties [the Allies] for political ends. Moreover, the German government would feel singled out and would undoubtedly do two things: it would make the persecution harsher against the Catholic Poles, and it would prevent the Holy See from having any contacts in any way with the Polish bishops and from carrying out the charitable work that it can now carry out, albeit in a less forceful fashion.[63]

What do the historians make of all this? Falconi cites numerous articles in the clandestine Polish press complaining about the papal silence, and concludes that Pius' "blind trust in diplomacy" led him to ignore the Polish requests.[64] Michael Phayer says that Sapieha's and the other Polish bishops' waning criticism of Pius' silence after the winter of 1942–43 was the result of a change on Nazi policy toward the Poles, and had nothing to do with the Pope's diplomacy: before the German surrender at Stalingrad, the Germans were intent upon suppressing the Poles; after Stalingrad, they wanted to "utilize the church to mobilize the Polish people against Communist Russia."[65] Robert Graham uses the Vatican documents to point out the bishops' frustration, but concludes that in the end, they all came around to support the Pope's position. He points out that Bishop Radonski's complaints "were an explosion of grief and frankness [which] provided, by his filial remonstrations, his own witness to [his] solidarity with the Holy See."[66] It is difficult to see how Graham arrives at that conclusion.

63. 18 May 1942, *ADSS* 3:569–70.
64. *Silence*, 225–35, 93.
65. *Catholic Church*, 29.
66. *The Pope and Poland*, 14.

Croatia

When the Germans invaded Yugoslavia in the spring of 1941, the country broke up into its constituent ethnic entities. In the north, the new state of Croatia was proclaimed and the fascist Ustasha took control of the country. Its leader, Ante Pavelic, established a favored role for the Church, an action met with great enthusiasm by the Church hierarchy. Croat politicians made fervent statements that Croat nationalism was consubstantial with Catholicism.

Undoubtedly the Pope was pleased with this event. Ever since the establishment of the Yugoslav state in 1919, Croatian Catholics had felt discriminated against by the Orthodox Serbs who dominated the government of Yugoslavia. The new Croat state would, they felt, give Catholics a rightful place in the society and government of the area.

But few clerics, including the Pope, were aware of the fact that Pavelic was setting out upon a campaign of ethnic and religious persecution against the Orthodox Serbs in Croatia, a group that numbered 2.2 million against the 3.3 million Croats (there were also 350,000 Muslims and 45,000 Jews in the new state). In the early, heady days of the new state, the bishops proclaimed their enthusiastic support of the new regime. The Archbishop of Zagreb, Alojzije Stepinac, was particularly supportive—until he found out after a few months that the Ustasha was determined upon a policy of forced conversions of the Orthodox Serbs, and worse, systematic killings of both those who would not convert and of the Serb middle class as well. A number of priests were among the persecutors. However, Stepinac made no public protest against the Ustasha terror.[67]

---

67. See Stella Alexander, *The Triple Myth: A Life of Archbishop Alojzije Stepinac* (New York: Columbia University Press, 1987).

As for Pope Pius' reaction to these events, when Pavelic traveled to Rome, hoping for the blessing of the Pope on his new regime, he was told that Vatican policy was to refrain from establishing diplomatic relations with states that had been created in wartime because of their impermanence. (This was technically true, but the Vatican had established relations with Slovakia after the breakup of Czechoslovakia six months before the outbreak of World War II, and it maintained relations with Vichy France, presumably viewing the puppet state as a continuation of the French Republic.) Pavelic was received by the Pope, not as the head of state, but rather as a private citizen, and thereafter there were Croatian complaints about the lack of recognition. The Pope named an apostolic minister to Croatia, Giuseppe Marcone, who was treated by Pavelic as if he were a nuncio.[68]

The bishops protested the forced conversions of Serbs; they were informed that the state would continue them; the bishops then said that it was a violation of church doctrine that the state should be in charge of the conversions, that such action properly belonged to the clergy. The Pope backed them up, writing to them in November 1941, telling them to "hold to the principle that everything which might hinder the free and willing return of the Orthodox to the Catholic Church might be avoided."[69]

Why did the Pope not make a public protest of the horrifying slaughter of hundreds of thousands of Serbs that accompanied the forced conversions? Why did he give scandal by receiving the bloody dictator Pavelic in Rome? Owen Chadwick says that "the Pope did not believe the stories about Pavelic."[70] Michael O'Carroll, Pius' most ardent defender, says that the Vatican was so taken by the speed of events in Croatia that the Pope did not want to rebuff Pavelic; and furthermore, that information

68. 16–18 May 1941, *ADSS* 4:491–92, 495.
69. Cited in Alexander, 78.
70. *Britain and the Vatican*, 148.

on the forced conversions was not widely known until after the war. At that time it was released by the Communist Yugoslav state, which tried and sentenced Stepinac for collaboration with the Germans, so that naturally it wanted to put an anticlerical spin on the facts.[71]

But it does seem most unlikely that Pius did not know of the forced conversions. Falconi says that Pius was "more than [a] benevolent supporter of Ustasha Croatia." He cites meetings between the Pope and Croatian ministers in which the Pope said he "willingly imparts" his blessing on Pavelic as late as July 1943 when he had absolute knowledge of the slaughters in Croatia; Falconi contrasts this with Pius' clear condemnation of the Soviet slaughter in June 1945 at the beginning of the Soviet occupation.[72] The most scathing criticism of the Pope in his dealings with the Ustasha comes from Edmond Paris,[73] but here the documentation backing up his statements comes largely from the Croatian Catholic press, which naturally would want to portray the Pope as supporting the Ustasha.

Michael Phayer has one of the soundest criticisms of the Vatican's policy toward Croatia. He argues that while the Pope was truly horrified by the events in Croatia, he did not want to criticize directly, preferring instead to work diplomatically to lessen the persecutions. His reason for doing so was to preserve the creation of a Catholic state in the Balkans. Phayer says, "The Holy See lost an opportunity to condemn genocide . . . just months before the Holocaust began. . . . The summer of 1941 would have been the right moment in time for the Holy See to exercise moral leadership."[74]

Added to the massacre of some 350,000 Orthodox Serbs and

---

71. *Pius XII*, 143–44.

72. *Silence*, 344, 350, 351.

73. *Genocide in Satellite Croatia, 1941–1945*, trans. Lois Perkins (Chicago: The American Institute for Balkan Affairs, n.d.).

74. *Catholic Church*, 39.

the forced conversion of another 300,000, was the deportation to the death camps of perhaps 9,00 Jews, and the arrest and death of most of the remaining Jews by the Ustashe.[75] The Apostolic Visitor, Marcone, did protest the arrest of baptized Jews and those married to Catholics, and this prevented their deportation, for the most part. Morley concludes his discussion of the Vatican's relations with Croatia by saying that "the record of Croatia on the Jews is particularly shameful . . . because it was a state that proudly proclaimed its Catholic tradition and whose leaders depicted themselves as loyal to the Church and to the Pope."[76]

Another criticism of papal silence goes beyond the war. When Germany, and perforce the Croat state, collapsed in 1945, Pavelic went into hiding first in Austria and then in Italy, where he was given support by some Vatican officials.[77] Michael Phayer argues that Pius probably knew of the aid given not only Pavelic, but also other Ustasha criminals; Montini, the papal undersecretary of state, certainly knew because of his contacts with Croatian clerics in Rome, and since Montini reported to the Pope daily, Phayer claims Pius must have known; but since the British were equally culpable in allowing Ustasha criminals to escape in the climate of the Cold War, it is difficult to make a judgment, given "the historical context of postwar Rome and Europe."[78]

Of all the criticisms of Pius during World War II, his behavior toward the events in Croatia are the most damning. There were no extenuating circumstances that could have led him to keep silent, for he was dealing with a government that pro-

75. See Menachem Shelah, "The Catholic Church in Croatia, the Vatican, and the Murder of the Croatian Jews," *Holocaust and Genocide Studies* 4, no. 3 (1989): 323–39.

76. *Vatican Diplomacy*, 165.

77. See Mark Aarons and John Loftus, *Unholy Trinity* (New York: St. Martin's Press, 1991), 77ff.

78. *Catholic Church*, 172–73.

claimed itself Catholic, and there was no fear of retribution that might result from a papal protest.

Romania

There appears to be little criticism of the Pope in his relations with Romania. The papal nuncio, Andrea Cassulo, acted often and vigorously to protest the persecution of the Jews and to offer what help he could. Morley shows that much of Cassulo's protest was based on the concordat and that therefore he was protecting Jews who had converted to Catholicism. However, Cassulo also made protests concerning non-Catholic Jews and both he and Cardinal Maglione approved the mass conversions of Jews and asked for government protection of them.[79] Pius approved of these efforts on behalf of the Romanian Jews, for he sent sums of money to Cassulo to be used to alleviate the sufferings of the Jews.[80]

Slovakia

Slovakia was a predominately Catholic state. After it declared independence from Czechoslovakia under German pressure, a priest, Josef Tiso, became President of Slovakia. Pius was displeased with this situation, for Vatican policy had for years been opposed to the clergy taking on political roles. When the Slovaks began anti-Semitic persecutions, the Vatican chargé, Giuseppe Burzio, made numerous protests.[81] Morley criticizes

79. *Vatican Diplomacy*, 23–47.
80. Lapide, 167–68. Supporting these views is Theodore Lavi, "The Vatican's Endeavors on Behalf of Rumanian Jewry during the Second World War," *Yad Vashem Studies* 5 (1963): 405–18. See also Blet, *Pie XII*, 207–12.
81. See Livia Rothkirchen, "Vatican Policy and the 'Jewish Problem' in 'Independent' Slovakia (1939–1945)," *Yad Vashem Studies* 5 (1963): 405–18; John S. Conway, "The Churches, the Slovak State and the Jews 1939–1945," *Slavonic and East European Review* 52 (1974): 85–112; and Blet, *Pie XII*, 192–203.

the Pope for not taking the opportunity to protest himself, arguing that it would have had great effect in this Catholic country.[82] It was clear, however, that the Vatican was opposed to the persecutions. Tardini, the undersecretary of state, summed up Vatican efforts in a memorandum on Slovakia: "It is a great misfortune that the President of Slovakia is a priest. Everyone knows that the Holy See cannot bring Hitler to heel. But who will understand that we cannot even control a priest?"[83]

Hungary

After Poland and the Soviet Union, Hungary had the largest number of Jews in Europe. It was an ally of Germany, a member of the Axis Pact. Until 1944, the Hungarian Jews had not been subject to persecution. Then, in the spring of 1944, in response to an impending Soviet invasion, the Germans invaded and occupied Hungary. A pro-German government was set up and it began deporting Jews to the death camps. The Hungarian bishops protested. The nuncio, Angelo Rotta, protested.[84] Finally, in July 1944, Pope Pius sent a letter to the Premier, Nicholas Kállay, asking that he do everything in his power to prevent further persecution of the "unfortunate people" being persecuted because of "their nationality or racial origin."[85] The Premier was able to stop the deportations for a short time. In autumn, when the deportations began again, the World Jewish Congress sent a message to the Vatican asking that the Pope broadcast a radio appeal to stop the deportations. Pius did not issue a radio appeal;

---

82. *Vatican Diplomacy*, 101.

83. 13 July 1942, *ADSS* 8:598.

84. Moshe Y. Herczl, *Christianity and the Holocaust of Hungarian Jewry*, trans. Joel Lerner (New York: New York University Press, 1993), 200–203, interprets Rotta's protests as applying only to those Jews converted to Catholicism.

85. The text of the letter is published in Jeno Levai, *Hungarian Jewry and the Papacy*, trans. J. R. Foster (London: Sands and Co., 1968), 26.

rather, he sent a message to Cardinal Justinian Seredi, the Hungarian primate, declaring that he supported the bishops' efforts to assist "all victims of the war, regardless of their race."[86] The Germans continued their deportations and most of the Hungarian Jews were killed.

Jeno Levai, in his documentary study, concludes that Hitler's ignoring the papal appeal (for it was sent through regular channels and the Germans knew about it) is proof that a forthright papal protest would have had no effect upon the German plan to kill all of the European Jews.[87] Michael Phayer argues that the Pope was too late in making his appeal and did so only because of world pressure instigated by Protestant theologians, and he discounts the nuncio's protests, claiming that he acted "without instructions from the Holy See."[88]

Germany

The German bishops have come in for their share of criticism for both supporting Hitler's war and not coming out with a strong statement of protest against the destruction of the innocent, while at the same time making numerous protests against the Nazi regime's violations of the Reich Concordat and its treatment of the Church.[89] The concern here, however, is how

86. Cited in Blet, *Pie XII*, 223.

87. *Hungarian Jewry*, 112.

88. *Catholic Church*, 108. Randolph L. Braham, *The Politics of Genocide: The Holocaust in Hungary* (New York: Columbia University Press, 1981), 2:1063ff., also criticizes Pius, but his sources are secondary and rely largely upon Friedlander.

89. Gordon Zahn, *German Catholics and Hitler's Wars* (New York: E. P. Dutton, 1969); John S. Conway, *The Nazi Persecution of the Churches 1933–1945*, and Guenter Lewy, *The Catholic Church and Nazi Germany* are three seminal works on the topic. See also information on the clergy in the admirable study by Theodore Hamerow, *On the Road to the Wolf's Lair: German Resistance to Hitler* (Cambridge: Harvard University Press, 1997).

Pope Pius XII reacted to the German bishops' stance and to the Nazi regime as well.

The question of why he did not encourage them to protest their government's destruction of the innocent is at the center of the controversy of his alleged silence. The Bishop of Berlin, Konrad von Preysing, had asked him to make an appeal for the Jews.[90] Pius replied that he had decided to let the bishops be the judges of their own situations. In a response to Preysing on April 30, 1943, Pius elaborated on a number of themes that related to the destruction of the innocent and to relations with the German government. He said that he sympathized with the Bishop over the Allied bombing of Berlin and that he prayed daily for victims of aerial bombardment, but pointed out that he did so for those on both sides. He was sorry that the German government refused to allow the Vatican to inform the families of German prisoners of war of their whereabouts. He was pleased with the German bishops, and with Preysing's pastoral letters defending the rights "of the human person on behalf of those who are defenseless and who are oppressed by public authority, whether the victims are children of the Church or not." He further said that "it was a consolation for Us to learn that Catholics, notably in Berlin, had manifested great Christian charity toward the sufferings of 'non-Aryans'" in referring to Bernard Lichtenberg, the Berlin priest who had been outspoken in defense of the Jews and who consequently was arrested and died on his way to prison in Dachau. He then came to the crucial point, which was that he believed it best to leave to the bishops the "task of assessing whether, and to what extent, the danger of reprisals and pressures and, perhaps, other circumstances due to the length and the psychological climate of the war, counsel restraint—despite reasons that might exist for interven-

90. 17 January 1943, *ADSS* 9:82–83.

tion—in order to avoid greater evils. This is one of the motives for the limitations which We impose on Ourself in Our declarations." On the Jews, he said that "the Holy See has acted charitably, within the limits of its responsibilities, on the material and moral plane," and he said that he had disbursed large sums of American money for Jewish emigrants. He referred to his Christmas message of 1942 in which he had criticized the persecution of the Jews (though not by name): "It was short but it was well understood." He continued, "Unhappily, in the present circumstances, We cannot offer them effective help other than through Our prayers."[91]

This decision has been criticized by Michael Phayer and Frank Buscher. They say that such a policy played into the hands of those bishops, most notably Cardinal Adolf Bertram of Breslau, who hesitated to criticize the regime.[92] In his more recent study, Phayer says that "had the Vatican provided [the bishops] with the detailed information [about the Holocaust] at its disposal, the more timid bishops would, in all likelihood, have swung over to Preysing's confrontational stance."[93] But the decision still bothered Pius, for he later told the new archbishop of Cologne, Josef Frings, in March 1944, "Superhuman exertions . . . are necessary to keep the Holy See above parties [and] it is often painfully difficult to decide whether reticence and cautious silence are called for or frank speech and strong action: all this torments Us more bitterly than the threats to peace and security in Our own household."[94]

91. 30 April 1943, *ADSS* 2:318–27; English translation in Friedlander, *Pius XII*, 135–43.

92. "German Catholic Bishops and the Holocaust, 1940–1952," *German Studies Review* 11, no. 3 (October 1988): 469.

93. *Catholic Church*, 81.

94. 3 March 1944, *ADSS* 2:365, written at a time when Rome was under German occupation and there were strong rumors of threats to the Pope.

Nor was Pius certain that his messages were getting through to the German people. In March 1942, he wrote to Preysing that although his Christmas message of 1941 was heard throughout the world, "We learn with sadness that it was almost completely hidden from the hearing of German Catholics."[95]

A chief point of criticism of the Pope is his unwillingness to replace Cesare Orsenigo as his nuncio to Berlin. As Chadwick says, "The Pope knew how weak with the Nazis he was. The Pope was a personal friend of Preysing, the tough Catholic Bishop of Berlin; and Preysing's opinion of Orsenigo was none too episcopal. Yet the Pope kept Orsenigo in Berlin throughout the war. Was it that anybody in Berlin was better than nobody, and if he recalled Orsenigo he would never be allowed to send a replacement? Or did it suit his still nature to keep, as responsible for papal relations with Nazis, a clergyman so likely to put up with whatever happened?"[96] Phayer and Morley both criticize the Pope for keeping Orsenigo on in this crucial diplomatic post.[97] However, Blet argues that the diplomatic bag from the nunciature to Rome was the only certain way for the German bishops to communicate with the Pope. If he dismissed Orsenigo and the German government refused to recognize a new nuncio, this vital means of communication would be lost.[98]

Pius has been criticized for singling out Hitler as the first government leader to officially notify of his election as Pope in March 1939, and of sending a personal letter to the German dictator. Some critics see this as a sign of favor.[99] However, others have pointed out that Pius wanted to show Hitler that he did not

95. 1 March 1942, *ADSS* 2:253.

96. Pius XII: The Legends and the Truth," 401.

97. Morley, 126–28, and Phayer, *Catholic Church*, 44ff. See also the defense of Orsenigo in Biffi, 283.

98. *Pie XII*, 75–76.

99. Friedlander, *Pius XII*, 10ff.

have Pius XI's temperament and he wanted to negotiate a settlement of outstanding problems, and that furthermore, he did so at the urging of the German cardinals who had stayed in Rome after the papal election.[100]

Perhaps the most scandalous action of the Pope in this regard was his sending Hitler a telegram expressing his "deep satisfaction" at the German dictator's narrowly escaping an assassination attempt in 1939.[101] It should be noted that this message came two months after the Germans had started the war and at a time when the Pope was already aware of German atrocities in Poland—and ironically at the same time that he had offered his services as a conduit to those anti-Hitler Germans who wanted to contact the British to arrange peace terms. Similarly, after the July 20, 1944, attempt on Hitler's life, Orsenigo, the nuncio, delivered congratulations in the name of the Holy See upon Hitler's successful escape. Blet points out that in both cases, the entire diplomatic corps congratulated Hitler, as was traditional in the case of an attempt upon the life of a head of state; that it was simply a *pro forma* diplomatic communication.[102]

Furthermore, Pius privately, and *L'Osservatore Romano* publicly, criticized the Soviets by name for the invasion of Finland in 1939 but did not criticize Germany by name for any of its aggressions. Nor did the Pope condemn the bombing of Britain by the Germans, but he did condemn the Allied bombing of Ger-

100. Lewy, 220; see also John Zeender, "Germany: The Catholic Church and the Nazi regime, 1933–1945," in *Catholics, the State and the European Radical Right, 1919–1945,* ed. R. J. Wolff and J. K. Hoensch (New York: Columbia University Press, 1987), 104. This was not the first time a pope had so favored a hostile government. Benedict XV notified the French government first of his election in 1914, as a means of conciliation after two decades of tension.

101. See *The New York Times,* 11 Nov 1939, 2:14, and *L'Osservatore Romano,* 11 November 1939, 1, for its commentary on the event.

102. Blet, *Pie XII,* 294.

many to the German bishops. Chadwick says that Osborne, the British Minister at the Vatican, had to persuade Pius to send a note of congratulation to the British monarchs on their escape from a German bombing of Buckingham Palace in 1940.[103] Of course, it can be argued that there were few Catholics in the Soviet Union to persecute if Stalin took umbrage at the papal protest (and the Soviets had been persecuting Catholics for years), and British Catholics were in a distinct minority, while there were more than 20 million Catholics in Germany, and many more in the occupied countries. But these acts do serve, I believe, to indicate a concern with the well-being of German Catholics that derived from Pius' long experience as nuncio to Bavaria and Germany. Historian Léon Papeleux argues that because of this concern for Germans, Pius favored them during the war, and this affected his claimed impartiality.[104]

Finally there are the charges that Pius purposely kept a blind eye to the help given Nazi war criminals after 1945 by some Vatican officials who provided them with false passports and allowed them to use the facilities of the Vatican. While it is known that Alois Hudal, the rector of the German seminary in Rome, was helping such persons, how much Pius knew of this is disputed. Phayer claims, based on American occupation authorities' documents, that the Vatican was helping Nazi war criminals. But while he says repeatedly that Pius closed his eyes to this activity, at the same time, he notes that "we cannot say that the pope himself . . . knew [that some of the persons helped] had been central figures in carrying out the Holocaust . . . but [he] had every reason to suspect it." He argues that Pius appointed the pro-Nazi Hudal as rector of the German seminary in Rome, knowing that from this position Hudal would come into contact

103. *Britain and the Vatican,* 137.
104. *Les Silences,* 265.

with the Nazi criminals and would aid them: "We may conclude that at the very least the Holy See allowed an environment to exist in Rome through which fugitives from justice could escape to foreign lands."[105] Jesuit Pierre Blet claims that the charges are false and that Pius knew nothing of Hudal's activity.[106]

105. *Catholic Church*, 169.
106. "La Leggenda," 539.

Chapter 15

Conclusion
A Pathetic and Tremendous Figure

In the fall of 1944, after the liberation of Rome by the Allies, Harold Macmillan, then the British High Commissioner on the Allied Advisory Council for Italy, paid an official visit to Pope Pius XII. He reported that he found "a sense of timelessness—time means nothing here, centuries come and go, but this is like living in a sort of fourth dimension. And at the centre of it all, past the papal guards, and the monsignori, and the bishops, and the cardinals, and all the show of ages—sits the little saintly man, rather worried, obviously quite selfless and holy—at once a pathetic and tremendous figure."[1]

Whatever Macmillan meant by his observation, it fits Pius well. Pathetic because he could do nothing to lessen the horror of the war. As the Vicar of Christ, he had the charge to act as Christ for humanity, and in his judgment that responsibility did not include the response his critics say he should have made. The burden of his office to care for the Church, along with his belief that a public protest

1. *The Blast of War, 1939–1945* (New York: Harper and Row, 1968), 460.

would make things worse, would not, in his mind, allow him to make a strong condemnation of Nazi Germany. And tremendous because he had, for Catholics the world over, the spiritual power to lead them to salvation. These two duties—Vicar of Christ and leader of the Church—he found impossible to reconcile in order to satisfy the critics that would come to judge his wartime role.

The subject of Pius XII and the Holocaust has become one of the most contentious arguments in recent history. Many of the journalists and historians who have written on the subject are no closer to agreement today than they were after Hochhuth's drama was produced in 1963. It is indeed a testament to the strength of the argument that John Cornwell's *Hitler's Pope,* despite its many shortcomings, was on bestseller lists shortly after it was published in September 1999. In one sense, the argument over Pius has less to do with his alleged silence and more to do with his diplomacy; for, if he had been successful in rescuing large numbers of Jews and other innocent victims, then his silence would have been justified. Indeed, this is the argument made by his defenders; unfortunately, they have no way of documenting the numbers of those who were in fact saved by papal intervention.

In the end, what conclusions can be drawn from the long and protracted debate on Pius' role in the Holocaust? Of the various arguments advanced by critics and defenders, some appear less convincing than others.

The claim that Pius was an anti-Semite and therefore uninterested in the fate of the Jews stems mainly from his identity as the leader of a church that had promoted anti-Semitism down through the ages; but as an individual, the claim has little factual basis. The specific charge that he was interested only in Jews who had converted to Catholicism is explained by the fact that the Church had a better legal basis to protect those converts. The charge is furthermore not tenable in view of his direct intervention with the Hungarian regent, urging protection for the Jews, and his instruction to his nuncios in the German satellite states to do so as well. He offered to lend the Roman Jews the gold to pay the ransom demanded by the German occupiers. Although specific documentation is lacking, it appears most likely that he directed Italian clergy to open their convents and monasteries to the hunted Jews, and in fact he did open the Vatican's properties to them.

The contentions that the Pope's fear that Rome would suffer destruction and that the security of the Vatican would be jeopardized if he made a strong protest does not appear to have much substance. The persecution of the Jews began long before Italy became involved in the war, and the Nazi death camps were operating more than a year before the Germans occupied Rome and the city was the target of Allied bombs. Pius did not make a strong protest before he began to fear destruction of Rome or to be concerned for the security of the Vatican; thus concern for Rome's safety does not seem to have been an important reason for his behavior.

The argument that Pius feared that a protest would lead to the Nazi government's unilateral abrogation of the German concordat and leave German Catholics open to persecution by the Nazi regime appears to have some substance. As long as the concordat remained in force, although violated by the government, there was an avenue of complaint through the nuncio. The Pope himself claimed after the war that the concordat, which he had helped to negotiate as papal Secretary of State, provided a basis for the defense of German Catholics. In view of the fact that Pius believed that a public protest was unlikely to be allowed to circulate in Germany or to have any salutary effect upon the Nazi machine of destruction, protection of Germany's Catholics through the provisions of the concordat does appear to have been a factor in Pius' behavior.

While Vatican diplomacy has not always been cautious, Pius' training as a diplomat led him to exercise caution in his dealings with the Nazi regime and was unquestionably a factor in his response to the Holocaust, although his agreeing to serve as a conduit for secret talks between German dissidents and the British government shortly after the war broke out proves that he was not as discreet as he is often made out to be. Combined with the other rationales for his behavior, the argument that a different pope with a different training and outlook would have been more open to a strong protest against the Germans appears to have substance, although the traditional anachronistic approach of Vatican diplomats might have limited such a pope.

One of the most persistent arguments of Pius' critics is that he feared Soviet Communism more than German Nazism and therefore saw Nazi Germany as a bulwark against Soviet expansion. This argument lacks substance in view of Pius' stated refusal to condemn German atrocities because he would then have to condemn Soviet ones as well and therefore hurt the Allied war effort. There was also his response to the American bishops, who were concerned that Pius XI's strictures against Communism would prevent American Catholics from supporting Franklin Roosevelt's Lend-Lease aid to the Soviets; he told the bishops that it was possible to distinguish between aid to the Soviet people, which was legitimate, and aid to the Communist regime, which was not, and Lend-Lease fell under the first distinction. Furthermore, he refused to give in to German appeals to call the invasion of the Soviet Union a Christian crusade.

One of the critics' claims running through all their arguments is that Pius favored Germany because of his years in Germany as nuncio, his selection of Germans as his household staff and advisors, and his general predilection for things German. There is no question that Pius admired the German romantic cultural tradition, but it is a far reach to argue from this that he liked the Nazi government. He did see Germany as a bastion of Western culture against Soviet atheistic expansion, but he did not consider Nazism as part of that cultural tradition.

Another frequently argued contention is that Pius did not want to create a crisis of conscience for German Catholics, to force them to choose between their state and their faith, because he judged that most would choose their state, which had greater power of forcing compliance than their church. This argument may have some substance. German Catholics, indeed, common folk everywhere, would not be able to defy an omnipotent totalitarian state. On the other hand, the argument can go the other way, i.e., would Hitler have risked the support of one-third the population of Germany by forcing a showdown with the Pope? It appears that neither man was willing to push the other to the brink. The contention that with papal support, German Catholics would have deserted the regime *en masse,* flies in the face of the facts. There was no discernible opposition to Hitler's regime from Catholics in the wake of Pius XI's denunciation of the godless nature of Nazism in his 1937 encyclical, *Mit Brennender Sorge.* But the unknown effect of a forthright denunciation of the Nazi regime appears to have been a factor in Pius' decision not to make one.

The argument that Pius wanted to maintain a neutral stance so as to be in a position to mediate an end to the war also appears to have some substance. While it seems to have been a futile effort in view of both the Allies' doctrine of unconditional surrender and Hitler's bunker mentality, Pius' belief that he could serve in this role has to be viewed in the context of the events of the war. German opponents of Hitler attempted to assassinate the dictator more than once, most notably in the July 20, 1944, plot. If they had succeeded and asked for an armistice on the condition that they be allowed to govern a Nazi-less Germany and give up German gains, would the Allies have maintained their position of accepting nothing less than unconditional surrender? Was it unreasonable of Pius to believe that a group overthrowing Hitler's regime would have some hope of negotiating a compromise peace? And if so, would not the Pope be in a strong position to mediate that peace? That the Pope wanted to keep all avenues of mediation open certainly seems to be a factor in his aim to maintain neutrality in the conflict by not openly denouncing the German government.

The strongest argument for Pius' response is that he did not want to make things worse. He said so in private to diplomats and in public to the College of Cardinals. He believed that quiet diplomacy and private action would save more lives than public protest. His critics argue that nothing could have been worse than the Holocaust, that the Germans were determined to kill all of the Jews, and that therefore a papal protest might have had an effect. This argument ignores the fact that during the war, few people outside of the Nazi hierarchy knew that the Germans intended to kill *all* of the Jews. Did the Pope know this? Even if he been told of it, did he believe it possible, or even comprehensible? Owen Chadwick says: "Like the minds of most of western Europe, the mind of the Pope was not bad enough to believe the truth. . . . He thought that the Poles and the Jews exaggerated [their losses] for the sake of helping the war effort."[2] Thus, believing that Nazi aims were limited, Pius feared the effect of a protest on those who had not yet been harmed by the Germans—protected Jewish converts to Catholicism, priests in Dachau, the vast majority of Polish Catholics, and the half- and quarter-Jews who had not yet been killed.

In her analysis of the Pope's actions in Italy, Susan Zuccotti consistently argues that Pius and the other Vatican officials could have done more to help the Jews. This is undoubtedly true, but at what cost? Facing the horror of a moral calculation, the Pope

2. *Britain and the Vatican*, 218.

made choices that his critics perhaps would not have made; but it is easy to second-guess decades after the events. Given the circumstances of World War II, can we even understand the excruciating moral problems that the Nazi evil forced upon people, both high and low?

It is easy to criticize both defenders and critics, to take a middle position and argue that both are extremists. In fact, most of the Pope's critics tend to extremism, while defenders tend toward moderation. This is because the critics have taken the position that the Holocaust would have been much diminished, or even averted, by strong papal action, while defenders of the Pope argue more convincingly that a strong papal protest would have had little effect upon the Nazi machine of destruction.

Unfortunately, many defenders have adopted a pietistic tone, exacerbated by a sickly adulation and combined with outrage that their pope should be so attacked.[3] Some also charge that the critics are anti-Catholic, which perhaps some are, but that charge alone does not justify rejecting or exaggerating the historical facts.

Moderate defenders, like John Pawlikowski, argue that more research is necessary to get at the truth.[4] Certainly, the Holy See should allow qualified scholars access to the archives; but there is no guarantee that this will produce less biased works. Cornwell persuaded the Jesuits that he was qualified to examine the documents gathered for the beatification of Pius; he used some of the trivia he found to attack the Pope.

What seems apparent is that throughout the years of contro-

3. See, most notably, Margherita Marchione, *Pope Pius XII: Architect for Peace* (New York: Paulist Press, 2000), and the interesting but uneven and in part poorly documented work by Ronald Rychlak, *Hitler, the War, and the Pope.*

4. "The Catholic Response to the Holocaust: Institutional Perspectives," in *The Holocaust and History: The Known, the Unknown, the Disputed and the Reexamined,* ed. M. Berenbaum and A. J. Peck (Bloomington: Indiana University Press, 1998), 565–64.

versy, the critics of Pius (and his defenders, less so) have tended to make their judgments less on the basis of an impartial reading of the documents than on their preconceived sentiments. This situation probably will not change. Pius remains an alluring target for those opposed to clericalism or the papacy or the Church or the clergy, or simply to authoritarian systems.

What makes the controversy so contentious is that it deals with the most horrifying event of modern times. Who can blame a survivor of the Holocaust, such as Friedlander, for criticizing the Vicar of Christ for not speaking out forcefully against the Nazi machine of destruction, emanating from a Germany that was long one of the bastions of Christianity? For those wanting to place blame, it is tempting to overlook the fact that the Germans were the instigators of the Holocaust and to criticize the bystanders—the Allies, the neutrals, and above all the papacy—for not preventing it. What the Allies and the neutral nations lack is the single individual in charge upon whom the blame can be placed; what the papacy has is the single individual, who furthermore claimed to be the Vicar of Christ. Add to this Pius' personality and the impression he gave of omniscience, and it is easy to see why he has become a target of the critics. It is one of the great ironies of history that two persons with opposite temperaments and ideologies are paired together in this modern horror: Adolf Hitler, whom some see as the individual solely responsible for the Holocaust, and Pope Pius, singled out in similar fashion as the sole person who could have prevented or lessened its terrors.

Bibliography

Aarons, Mark, and John Loftus. *Unholy Trinity*. New York: St. Martin's Press, 1991.

Actes et Documents du Saint Siège relatifs à la Seconde Guerre mondiale. Edited by Pierre Blet, SJ, Burkhart Schneider, SJ, Angelo Martini, SJ, and Robert Graham, SJ. 11 Volumes. Vatican City: Libreria Editrice Vaticana, 1965–1981. Abbreviated *ADSS* throughout.

Alexander, Stella. *The Triple Myth: A Life of Archbishop Alojzije Stepinac.* New York: Columbia University Press, 1987.

Alvarez, David. "The Vatican and the Fall of Poland" In *The Opening of the Second World War,* edited by David W. Pike. New York: Peter Lang, 1991.

Alvarez, David, and Robert A. Graham, SJ. *Nothing Sacred: Nazi Espionage against the Vatican, 1939–1945.* London: Frank Cass, 1997.

Bea, Augustine. *The Unity of Christians.* New York: Herder and Herder, 1963.

Bentley, Eric, ed. *The Storm over the Deputy.* New York: Grove, 1964.

Biffi, Monica M. *Mons. Cesare Orsenigo: Nunzio Apostolico in Germania (1930–1946).* Milan: NED, 1997.

Biesinger, Joseph A. "The Reich Concordat of 1933." In *Controversial Concordats,* edited by Frank J. Coppa. Washington: The Catholic University of America Press, 1999.

Blet, Pierre, SJ. "La leggenda alla prova degli archive: le ricorrenti accuse contro Pio XII." *La Civiltà Cattolica* 3456 (1998): 531–41. English translation: Pius XII and the Second World War according to the Archives of the Vatican. Translated by Lawrence J. Johnson. New York: Paulist Press, 1999.

———. *Pie XII et la Seconde Guerre mondiale d'après les archives du Vatican.* Paris: Perrin, 1997.

Braham, Randolph L. *The Politics of Genocide; The Holocaust in Hungary.* Vol. 2. New York: Columbia University Press, 1981.

The Catholic Mind. 1939–1945.

Chadwick, Owen. *Britain and the Vatican during the Second World War.* Cambridge: Cambridge University Press, 1986.

———. "The Papacy and World War II." *Journal of Ecclesiastical History* 18, no. 1 (April 1967): 71–79.

———."Pius XII: The Legends and the Truth." *The Tablet,* 28 March 1998, 400–401.

———. "The Pope and the Jews in 1942." In *Persecution and Toleration,* edited by W. J. Sheils. London: Basil Blackwell, 1984.

———. Review of Volume 5 of *ADSS, Journal of Ecclesiastical History* 21, no. 3 (1970): 279–80.

———. "Weizsäcker, the Vatican, and the Jews of Rome." *Journal of Ecclesiastical History* 28, no. 2 (April 1977): 179–99.

Charles-Roux, François. *Huit ans au Vatican, 1932–1940.* Paris: Flammarion, 1947.

Cianfarra, Camille. *The War and the Vatican.* London: Burns, Oates, & Washbourne, 1945.

Commission for Religious Relations with the Jews. "We Remember: A Reflection on the Shoah." *The New York Times,* 17 March 1988, 10.

Conway, John S. "Catholicism and the Jews during the Nazi Period and After." In *Judaism and Christianity under the Impact of National Socialism,* edited by Otto Dov Kulka and Paul R. Mendes-Flohr. Jerusalem: The Historical Society of Israel and the Zalman Shazar Center for Jewish History, 1987.

———. "The Churches, the Slovak State and the Jews 1939–1945." *Slavonic and East European Review* 52 (1974): 85–112.

———. "The Meeting between Pope Pius XII and Ribbentrop." *Historical Papers of the Canadian Historical Association* 1 (1968): 215–27.

———. *The Nazi Persecution of the Churches.* New York: Basic Books, 1968.

———. "Records and Documents of the Holy See Relating to the Second World War." *Yad Vashem Studies* 15 (1983): 327–46.

———. "The Silence of Pope Pius XII." *Review of Politics* 27, no. 1 (January 1965): 105–31.

———. "The Vatican and the Holocaust: A Reappraisal." *Miscellanea Historiae Ecclesiasticae* 9 (1984): 475–89.

———. "The Vatican, Germany and the Holocaust." In *Papal Diplomacy in the Modern Age,* edited by P. Kent and J. F. Pollard. Westport, Conn.: Praeger, 1994.

Conzemius, Victor. *Eglises chretiennes et totalitarisme national-socialiste: un bi-*

lan historiographique. Louvain: Publications universitaires de Louvain, 1969.

―――. "Le Saint-Siège pendant la IIe guerre mondiale." *Miscellanea Historiae Ecclesiasticae* 9 (1984): 451–75.

Coppa, Frank J. "The Hidden Encyclical of Pius XI against Racism and Anti-Semitism Uncovered—Once Again!" *Catholic Historical Review* 84, no. 1 (January 1998): 63–72.

Cornwell, John. *Hitler's Pope: The Secret History of Pius XII.* New York: Viking, 1999.

d'Ormesson, Wladimir. *De Saint-Pétersbourg à Rome.* Paris: Plon, 1969.

Deak, Istvan. "The Pope, the Nazis and the Jews." *New York Review of Books,* 23 March 2000, 44–48.

de Lubac, Henri. *Christian Resistance to Anti-Semitism: Memories from 1940–1944.* Translated by Sister Elizabeth Englund. San Francisco: Ignatius Press, 1990.

Deutsch, Harold. *The Conspiracy against Hitler in the Twilight War.* Minneapolis: University of Minnesota Press, 1968.

Dietrich, Donald J. "Historical Judgments and Eternal Verities." *Society* 20, no. 3 (1983): 31–35.

Documents on British Foreign Policy, 1919–1939. 2d Series, vol. 5. London: Her Majesty's Stationery Office, 1956.

Drapac, Vesna. *War and Religion: Catholics in the Churches of Occupied Paris.* Washington: The Catholic University of America Press, 1998.

Duce, Alessandro. *Pio XII e la Polonia (1939–1945).* Rome: Edizione Studium, 1997.

Durand, Andre. *From Sarajevo to Hiroshima: History of the International Committee of the Red Cross.* Geneva: Henry Dunant Institute, 1984.

Elie, Paul. "John Paul's Jewish Dilemma." *New York Times Magazine,* 26 April 1998, 34–39.

Falconi, Carlo. *The Silence of Pius XII.* Translated by Bernard Wall. Boston: Little, Brown, 1970.

Fattorini, Emma. *Germania e Santa Sede: Le nunziature de Pacelli tra la Grande guerra e la Repubblica di Weimar.* Bologna: Società editrice il Mulino, 1992.

Fisher, Eugene. " Foreword" In *Holocaust Scholars Write to the Vatican,* edited by H. J. Cargas. Westport, Conn.: Greenwood Press, 1998.

Friedlander, Saul. *Pius XII and the Third Reich: A Documentation.* Translated by Charles Fullman. New York: Knopf, 1966.

―――. *Nazi Germany and the Jews: The Years of Persecution, 1933–1939.* New York: HarperCollins, 1997.

Gariboldi, Giorgio Angelozzi. *Il Vaticano nella Seconda Guerra Mondiale.* Milan: Mursia, 1992.

———. *Pio XII, Hitler e Mussolini.* Milan: Mursia, 1988.

Garzia, Italo. *Pio XII e l'Italia nella seconda guerra mondiale.* Brescia: Morcelliana, 1988.

———. "Pope Pius XII, Italy and the Second World War." In *Papal Diplomacy in the Modern Age,* edited by P. Kent and J. F. Pollard. Westport, Conn.: Praeger, 1994.

Giovannetti, Alberto. *L'Action du Vatican pour la paix (Documents inédits: 1939–1940).* Translated by E. de Pirey. Paris: Fleurus, 1963.

Graham, Robert. "How to Manufacture a Legend." In *Pius XII and the Holocaust.* Milwaukee: Catholic League for Religious and Civil Rights, 1988.

———. "La Radio Vaticana tra Londra e Berlino." *La Civiltà Cattolica* 3014 (1976): 132–50.

———. *The Pope and Poland in World War II.* London: Veritas, n.d.

———. "Relations of Pius XII and the Catholic Community with Jewish Organizations." In *The Italian Refuge: Rescue of Jews during the Holocaust,* edited by Ivo Herzer. Washington: The Catholic University of America Press, 1989.

Greene, Graham. "The Pope Who Remains a Priest." *Life,* 24 September 1951, 146–62.

Grippenberg, G. A. "Recollections of Pius XII." *America,* 18 April 1964, 539–43.

Gumpel, Peter, SJ. "Cornwell's Pope: A Nasty Caricature of a Noble and Saintly Man." *Zenit News Service,* 16 September 1999.

Halecki, Oscar. *Pius XII—Pope of Peace.* New York: Creative Age Press, 1951.

Halls, W. D. *Politics, Society and Christianity in Vichy France.* Oxford: Berg, 1995.

Hamerow, Theodore. *On the Road to the Wolf's Lair: German Resistance to Hitler.* Cambridge: Harvard University Press, 1997.

Hebblethwaite, Peter. *In the Vatican.* Bethesda, Md.: Adler & Adler, 1968.

Herczl, Moshe Y. *Christianity and the Holocaust of Hungarian Jewry.* Translated by Joel Lerner. New York: New York University Press, 1993.

Hill, Leonidas. "History and Rolf Hochhuth's *The Deputy.*" In *From an Ancient to a Modern Theatre,* edited by R. G. Collins. Winnepeg: University of Manitoba Press, 1972.

———. "The Vatican Embassy of Ernst von Weizsäcker, 1943–1945." *Journal of Modern History* 39 (1967): 138–59.

Hitler's Secret Conversations, 1941–1944. Translated by N. Cameron and R. Stevens. New York: Farrar, Strauss, and Cudahy, 1953.

Hochhuth, Rolf. *The Deputy.* Translated by Richard and Clara Winston. New York: Grove, 1964.

Hurten, Heinz. *Deutsche Katholiken, 1918–1945.* Paderborn: F. Schöningh, 1992.

Kállay, Nicholas. *Hungarian Premier.* New York: Columbia University Press, 1954.

Katz, Robert. *Black Sabbath.* New York: Macmillan, 1969.

Kertzer, David. *The Kidnapping of Edgardo Mortara.* New York: Knopf, 1997.

Kessel, Albrecht von. "The Pope and the Jews." In *Storm over the Deputy,* edited by Eric Bentley. New York: Grove, 1964.

Kohler, Otto. "Der Streit um den Stellvertreter." In *Summa Iniuria oder Durfte der Papst schweigen?* edited by Fritz J. Raddatz. Hamburg: Rowohlt, 1964.

L'Osservatore Romano. 1933–1945.

LaFarge, John. *The Manner Is Ordinary.* New York : Harcourt, Brace, 1954.

Lapide, Pinchas. *Three Popes and the Jews.* New York: Hawthorn Books, 1967.

La Pira, Giorgio. "The Political Heritage of Pius XII." *Foreign Affairs* 18 (April 1940): 486–506.

Laqueur, Walter. *The Terrible Secret.* Boston: Little Brown, 1980.

Lavi, Theodore. "The Vatican's Endeavors on Behalf of Rumanian Jewry during the Second World War." *Yad Vashem Studies* 5 (1963): 405–18.

Lehnert, Pascalina. *Ich durfte ihm dienen: Erinnerungen an Papst Pius XII.* Würzburg: Verlag Johann Wilhelm Naumann, 1982.

Levai, Jeno. *Hungarian Jewry and the Papacy.* Translated by J. R. Foster. London: Sands and Co., 1968.

Lewy, Guenter. *The Catholic Church and Nazi Germany.* New York: McGraw-Hill, 1964.

Lieber, Robert, SJ. "Der Papst und die Verfolgung der Juden." In *Summa Iniuria oder Durfte der Papst schweigen?* edited by Fritz J. Raddatz. Hamburg: Rowohlt, 1964.

———. "Pius as I Knew Him." *The Catholic Mind* 57 (1959): 292–304.

———. "Pius XII +." *Stimmen der Zeit* 163 (1958–1959): 81–100.

———. "Pius XII und die Juden in Rom." *Stimmen der Zeit* 167 (1960–61): 428–36.

Lukacs, John. *The Last European War.* Garden City, N.Y.: Anchor/Doubleday, 1976.

Lukas, Richard. *The Forgotten Holocaust: The Poles under German Occupation 1939–1944.* Lexington: University Press of Kentucky, 1986.

Luxmoore, Jonathan, and Jolanta Babiuch. *The Vatican and the Red Flag: The Struggle for the Soul of Eastern Europe.* London: Geoffrey Chapman, 1999.

Macmillan, Harold. *The Blast of War, 1939–1945.* New York: Harper and Row, 1968.

Marchione, Margherita. *Pope Pius XII: Architect for Peace.* New York: Paulist Press, 2000.

Marrus, Michael R. *The Holocaust in History.* Hanover, N.H.: University Press of New England, 1987.

———, editor. *The Nazi Holocaust.* Vol. 8.3: *Bystanders to the Holocaust.* Westport, Conn.: Meckler, 1989.

———. "The Nuremberg Trial: Fifty Years After." *The American Scholar* 66 (Winter 1997): 563–70.

Marrus, Michael R., and Robert O. Paxton. *Vichy France and the Jews.* New York: Basic Books, 1981.

Martini, Angelo, SJ. "Il Cardinale Faulhaber e L'Enciclica 'Mit Brennender Sorge'." *Archivum Historiae Pontificiae* 2 (1964): 303–20.

McGurn, Barrett. *A Reporter Looks at the Vatican.* New York: Coward-McCann, 1962.

Miccoli, Giovanni. "Aspetti e problemi del pontificato de Pio XII a proposito de alcune pubblicazioni recenti." *Cristianesimo Nella Storia* 9 (1988): 343–427.

———. *I dilemmi e i silenzio di Pio XII.* Milan: Rizzoli, 2000.

Michaelis, Meir. "Christians and Jews in Fascist Italy." In *Judaism and Christianity under the Impact of National Socialism,* edited by Otto Dov Kulka and Paul R. Mendes-Flohr. Jerusalem: The Historical Society of Israel and the Zalman Shazar Center for Jewish History, 1987.

———."The Holocaust in Italy." In *The Holocaust in History: The Known, the Unknown, the Disputed, and the Reexamined,* edited by M. Berenbaum and A. J. Peck. Bloomington: Indiana University Press, 1998.

———. *Mussolini and the Jews.* Oxford: Clarendon Press, 1978.

Morley, John F. *Vatican Diplomacy and the Jews during the Holocaust, 1939–1943.* New York: KYAV, 1980.

Moynihan, Robert. "The Pope Skips a Sentence." *Inside the Vatican,* August-September, 1996, 15.

The New York Times. 1939–1945.

Nobécourt, Jacques. *"Le Vicaire" et l'Histoire.* Paris: Editions du Seuil, 1964.

O'Carroll, Michael. *Pius XII: Greatness Dishonoured.* Chicago: Franciscan Herald Press, 1980.

Papée, Kazimierz. *Pius XII a Polska.* Rome: Editrice Studium, 1954.

Papeleux, Léon. *Les silences de Pie XII.* Brussels: Vokaer, 1980.

Paris, Edmund. *Genocide in Satellite Croatia, 1941–1945.* Translated by Lois Perkins. Chicago: The American Institute for Balkan Affairs, n.d.

Passelecq, Georges, and Bernard Suchecky. *The Hidden Encyclical of Pius XI.* Translated by S. Rendell. New York: Harcourt Brace, 1997.

Pawlikowski, John. "The Catholic Response to the Holocaust: Institutional Perspectives." In *The Holocaust and History: The Known, the Unknown, the Disputed and the Reexamined,* edited by M. Berenbaum and A. J. Peck. Bloomington: Indiana University Press, 1998.

————. "The Vatican and the Holocaust: Unresolved Issues." In *Jewish-Christian Encounters over the Centuries.* Edited by Marvin Perry and Frederick M. Schweitzer. New York: Peter Lang, 1994.

Phayer, Michael. *The Catholic Church and the Holocaust, 1930–1965.* Bloomington: Indiana University Press, 2000.

Phayer, Michael, and Frank Buscher. "German Catholic Bishops and the Holocaust, 1940–1952." *German Studies Review* 11, no. 3 (October 1988): 463–85.

Poliakov, Léon. "The Vatican and the 'Jewish Question': The Record of the Hitler Period—and After." *Commentary* 10 (November 1950): 439–49.

Pollard, John. *The Unknown Pope: Benedict XV.* London: Geoffrey Chapman, 1999.

————. *The Vatican and Italian Fascism, 1929–32.* Cambridge: Cambridge University Press, 1985.

Purdy, W. A. *The Church on the Move.* London: Hollis and Carter, 1966.

Raddatz, Fritz J., ed. *Summa Iniuria oder Durfte der Papst schweigen?* Hamburg: Rowohlt, 1964.

Rankin, Charles. *The Pope Speaks.* New York: Harcourt Brace, 1940.

Reitlinger, Gerald. *The Final Solution: The Attempt to Exterminate the Jews of Europe, 1939–1945.* New York: Beechhurst, 1953.

Repgen, Konrad. "German Catholicism and the Jews: 1933–1945." In *Judaism and Christianity under the Impact of National Socialism,* edited by Otto Dov Kulka and Paul R. Mendes-Flohr. Jerusalem: The Historical Society of Israel and the Zalman Shazar Center for Jewish History, 1987.

Rhodes, Anthony. *The Vatican in the Age of the Dictators (1922–1945).* New York: Holt, Rinehart and Winston, 1973.

Rothkirchen, Livia. "Vatican Policy and the 'Jewish Problem' in 'Independent' Slovakia (1939–1945)." *Yad Vashem Studies* 5 (1963): 405–18.

Rubenstein, Richard L. "A Twentieth-Century Journey." In *From the Unthinkable to the Unavoidable,* edited by Carol Rittner and John K. Roth. Westport, Conn.: Greenwood, 1997.

Rubinstein, William D. *The Myth of Rescue.* New York: Routledge, 1997.

Ruhm von Oppen, Beate. "Nazis and Christians." *World Politics* 21, no. 3 (1969): 392–424.

Rychlak, Ronald. *Hitler, the War, and the Pope.* Columbus, Miss.: Genesis Press, 2000.

Scholder, Klaus. *The Churches and the Third Reich.* Vol. 1. Translated by John Bowden. Philadelphia: Fortress Press, 1988.

Scrivener, Jane (pseud.). *Inside Rome with the Germans.* New York: Macmillan, 1945.

Sereny, Gitta. *Into That Darkness.* New York: McGraw Hill, 1974.

Shelah, Menachem. "The Catholic Church in Croatia, the Vatican, and the Murder of the Croatian Jews." *Holocaust and Genocide Studies* 4, no. 3 (1989): 323–39.

Stehlin, Stewart. *Weimar and the Vatican 1919–1933.* Princeton: Princeton University Press, 1983.

Tardini, Domenico. *Memories of Pius XII.* Translated by Rosemary Goldie. Westminster Md.: Newman Press, 1961.

Thavis, John. "Pope's Theologian: 'I Am Saddened.'" *Inside the Vatican,* April 1998, 32.

United States Department of State. *Foreign Relations of the United States: Diplomatic Papers 1942.* Washington: United States Government Printing Office, 1961.

Van Hoek, Kees. *Pope Pius XII, Priest and Statesman.* New York: Philosophical Library, n.d.

"Vatican Historian comes to Pius XII's Defense." *National Catholic Reporter.* 22 October, 1999, 14.

Veneruso, Danilo. "Pio XII e la Seconda Guerra Mondiale." *Revista di storia della chiesa in Italia* 22 (1968): 506–53.

Volk, Ludwig. *Kirchliche Akten über die Reichskonkordatsverhandlugen 1933.* Mainz: Matthias Grunewald Verlag, 1969.

Ward, W. R. "Guilt and Innocence: The German Churches in the Twentieth Century." *Journal of Modern History* 68, no. 2 (June 1996): 398–426.

Weil, Lynne, et al. "Jewish Reactions Are Cool." *Inside the Vatican,* April 1998, 29.

Weisbord, Robert G., and Wallace P. Sillanpoa. *The Chief Rabbi, the Pope and the Holocaust.* New Brunswick, N.J.: Transaction Publishers, 1992.

Weiss, John. *Ideology of Death.* Chicago: Ivan R. Dee, 1996.

Weizsäcker, Ernst von. *Die Weizsäcker Papiere.* Edited by Leonidas E. Hill. Frankfurt: Allstein, 1974.

———. *Memoirs of Ernst von Weizsäcker.* Translated by John Andrews. Chicago: Henry Regnery, 1951.

Wills, Garry. "The Vatican Monarchy." *New York Review of Books,* 19 February 1998, 20–25.

Woodruff, Douglas. "Quest of Perfection: Some Personal Impressions of Pius XII." *The Tablet,* October 18, 1958, 330–31.

Yahil, Leni. *The Holocaust: The Fate of European Jewry, 1932–1945.* New York: Oxford University Press, 1990.

Zahn, Gordon. "Catholic Responses to the Holocaust." *Thought* 56 (June 1981): 153–62.

———. *German Catholics and Hitler's Wars.* New York: E. P. Dutton, 1969.

Zeender, John. "Germany: The Catholic Church and the Nazi Regime, 1933–1945." In *Catholics, the State and the European Radical Right, 1919–1945,* edited by R. J. Wolff and J. K. Hoensch. New York: Columbia University Press, 1987.

Zuccotti, Susan. *Under His Very Windows: The Vatican and the Holocaust in Italy.* New Haven: Yale University Press, 2000.

Index

Acta Apostolica Sedis, 156

Actes et Documents du Saint Siège relatifs à la Seconde Guerre mondiale (ADSS), 29–30

Albigensians, 72

Alfieri, Dino, Italian Ambassador to the Holy See, 76, 78, 114–15

Allies, terror bombing by, 9

Alvarez, David, historian, 109, 145

American bishops, concern about communism, 106, 175

"Angelic Shepherd," film about Pius XII, 121

Anti-Semitism as a reason for Pius XII's alleged silence, 70–75

Ardeatine Cave massacre, 147

Assisi, bishop of, 148

Badoglio, Marshal Pietro, Italian premier, 94

Baltic countries, 30

Bavaria, 1919 revolution, 81

Bavarian Soviet, 15, 72

Bea, Cardinal Augustin, Pius XII's confessor, 126

Belgium, 52

Benedict XV, Pope, 15, 121, 122; as diplomat, 91, 92, 108, 169 n100

Bentley, Eric, editor, 31

Beran, Josef, Cardinal Archbishop of Prague, 21

Bérard, Léon, Ambassador from France to the Holy See, report to Pétain, 23, 149–51

Berning, Wilhelm, Bishop of Osnabrück, 74

Blet, Pierre, SJ, historian, *Pie XII et la Seconde Guerre mondiale d'aprés les archives du Vatican,* defends Pius XII, 4, 7; editor of Vatican documents, 29, 34; on Pope's alleged anti-Semitism, 72–73; on German Catholics, 100–101; on Orsenigo and attempt on Hitler, 169; on "rat line," 171

B'nai B'rith, Anti-Defamation League, 6

Bolshevism, German bishops fear of, 81–82, 84. *See also* Communists

Bourdoux, Henry, journalist, 121

Brazil, visa project, 74, 75

Britain and the Vatican during the Second World War, see Chadwick, Owen

British bishops, 23

British blockade of the Continent, 55

British Catholics, 170

British propaganda, 78

Bubis, Ignatz, Jewish spokesman, 7

Burzio, Giuseppe, Vatican chargé in Slovakia, 163

Buscher, Frank, historian, 167

Casablanca Conference, doctrine of unconditional surrender, 20, 57

Cassulo, Andrea, nuncio to Romania, 163

Castelgandolfo, papal summer palace, 79; as harbor for Jews, 149

Catholic Center Party, German, 22, 82–86

Chadwick, Owen, historian, *Britain and the Vatican During the Second World War,* 7–8, 30; on papal knowledge of Holocaust, 44, 45; on Maglione and Pius XII, 66; on Soviet-Western alliance, 106; on papal mediation, 111–12; on Pope's personality, 123; on Italian *razzia,* 143–45; on Croatia, 160; on nuncio Orsenigo, 168; on Pope and British monarchs, 170; on enormity of Holocaust, 177. *See also* Osborne, D'Arcy

Charles-Roux, François, French Ambassador to the Holy See, 30

Cianfarra, Camille, *New York Times* correspondent in Rome, 121, 127
clergy in Europe in 1939, 137
Cold War, papal actions during, 21, 96
Commission for Religious Relations
with the Jews, 5. *See also,* "We Remember: A Reflection on the Shoah"
Communism and Communists, American
bishops concern over, 106, 175; papal condemnation of, 21, 24, 94–95,
96; papal fear of, 103, 105–7, 175.
See also Bolshevism
Concordat of 1933 with Germany, negotiation of, 16, 22, 82–89; terms of,
85; as criticism of Pius XII, 25,
131–32; Pope's defense of, 60; German ignoring terms of, 67, 154
Conway, John, historian, on criticism of
Pius XII, 2, 3; articles by, 36; on
Pope's knowledge of Holocaust, 45;
on German view of Pope, 48; on
converted Jews, 75; on concordat of
1933, 87; on German Catholics, 100;
on papal sympathy for Nazis, 106;
on papal mediation of war, 111, 112–
13; on Pope's motives, 118; on Pope's
refusal to join Protestants in relief
efforts, 134; on Roman *razzia,* 145
Conzemius, Victor, historian, on Pius
XII's style, 11; article by, 36; on papal diplomacy, 90; on Bérard report,
151
Cornwell, John, journalist-historian,
Hitler's Pope, 6 n11, 34, 173; criticism
of Pius XII, 4–5; claims of papal
anti-Semitism, 72; on Pope's negotiation of concordat of 1933, 83; on
use of documents, 178
Croatia, 19; as criticism of Pius XII, 23,
118; Pope's relations with, 159–63
Croatian bishops, 160
Czechoslovakia, 160

d'Ormesson, Wladimir, French Ambas-
sador to the Holy See, 11, 30
Dachau, priests in, 61
Deak, Istvan, historian, 73
The Deputy, see Hochhuth, Rolf
Deutsche Allegemeine Zeitung, 51
Dezza, Paolo, SJ, rector of Gregorian
University, 115

Dietrich, Donald J., historian, 100
Divini Redemptoris, see Pius XI
Drapac, Vesna, historian, 66
Dreyfus Affair, 71
Dutch Catholics, 133

Enabling Act, 84

Falconi, Carlo, historian, *The Silence of
Pius XII,* 33–34; on Pius XII's re-
sponse to threat, 78; on *Mit Brenen-
der Sorge,* 88; on papal solidarity
with Protestants, 134; on Poles, 158;
on Croatia, 161
Fattorini, Emma, historian, 34
Faulhaber, Michael, Cardinal Archbishop
of Munich, as author of *Mit Brenender Sorge,* 17 n1; and Hitler, 84; and
threat of German national church,
100; and Pius XII, 112
Finland, Soviet invasion of, 51, 52, 65
Fisher, Eugene J., historian, 9
Fontana, Riccardo, protagonist in *The
Deputy,* 26–27
Foxman, Abraham, Jewish spokeman, 6
France, fall of, 52–52, 55; request for papal support of Poland, 88; Vichy
regime, 19; anticlerical laws, 23, 91;
and Pius XII, 149–53; diplomatic relations with Holy See, 160. *See also*
Pétain
French bishops,151–52
Friedlander, Saul, historian, *Pius XII and
the Third Reich,* 32–33; on German
suppression of *Summi Pontificatus,* 50;
on persecutions, 88; on Pope's fear
of communism, 103, 105–7; on Roman *razzia,* 145; on Bérard report,
151; and Tisserant, 153; on Holocaust, 179
Frings, Josef, Archbishop of Cologne,
167

Gariboldi, Giorgio Angelozzi, historian,
35
Gasparri, Pietro, Cardinal Secretary of
State under Pius XI, 84
German bishops, favored by Pius XII,
23, 24; documents on, 30, 73; praised
by Pope, 61; support of war, 68,
99–100, 165; relations with pre-

Hitler German regimes, 81–82; opposition to Hitler, 82–83; support
for concordat, 82; support for Hitler,
84; regulation of in concordat, 85
German Catholics, 97–102
Germany, as occupying power, 49, 50,
54; bombing of Britain, 54; bombing of Warsaw, 52; death camps, 43,
60; invasion of Greece, 19; invasion
of Hungary, 164; invasion of Low
Countries, 19; invasion of Norway
and Denmark, 19; invasion of
Poland, 18; invasion of Soviet
Union, 20, 43, 54, 55, 56, 105, 106,
154; invasion of Yugoslavia, 19, 54;
non-aggression pact with Poland,
52; non-aggression pact with Soviet
Union, 18, 105; occupation of Italy
and Rome, 20–21, 58–59, 77,
79–80, 94, 141–49; occupation of
Poland, 114–15; ransom demand
from Roman Jews, 142; Weimar
regime, 82, 84
Gestapo, 50
Giovannetti, Alberto, historian, 35, 100
Goebbels, Josef, Nazi propaganda chief,
101
Graham, Robert, SJ, historian, defends
Pius XII, 4, 120; editor of Vatican
documents, 29; on papal duty, 37; on
papal language, 67; on Roman *razzia*, 145; on papal instruction to Italian bishops, 148; on Polish persecution, 158
Greene, Graham, writer, 2
Grippenberg, G. A., Finnish Ambassador
to the Holy See, 127
Gumpel, Peter, SJ, postulator of Pius
XII's cause for sainthood, 4

Halls, W. D., historian, 151–52
Hebblethwaite, Peter, historian, 124
Herzberg, Arthur, Jewish spokesman, 6
Hill, Leonidas, historian, 112
Hitler, Adolf, German dictator, 4; notified of papal election, 23, 168–169;
as baptized Catholic, 40; attitude toward papacy 67–68; plan to kidnap
Pius XII, 77–78, 79, 141, 144; and
concordat of 1933, 81–89; views on
mediation, 110, 145–46; assassination

attempt, 110–11, 176–77 and Vatican
message to, 169; Hochhuth's view
of, 132; aims on Poland, 154; knowl-
edge of papal appeal to Hungarian
bishops, 165
Hitler's Pope, see Cornwell, John
Hlond, August, Cardinal Archbishop of
Gniesno and Posen, 49, 62, 156
Hochhuth, Rolf, playwright, *The Deputy
(Der Stellvertreter)* 2, 3, 24–28, 31, 82,
115, 131–32, 133, 142, 144, 152
Hoeckman, Remi, Vatican writer, 7
Holy See, archives, 28–29, 34
Hudal, Alois, rector of German College
in Rome, 144; and "rat line," 170–71
Humani Generis Unitas, see Pius XI
Hungarian bishops, 165
Hungary, 23; papal relations with,
164–65

Innocent III, Pope, 72
International Red Cross, 120
Italian Communist Party, 21
Italian Hebrew Commission, 5
Italy, declaration of war on Allies, 19;
elections of 1948, 24, 94; invasion
of Greece, 54; prisoners of war, 54;
surrender to Allies, 58; German occupation of, 94, 141–49

Joan of Arc, 91
John Paul I, Pope, 12
John Paul II, Pope, 6, 126
John XXIII, Pope, 2, 4, 12, 122, 126, 130
Jong, Johannes de, Archbishop of
Utrecht, 117

Kállay, Nicholas, Hungarian premier,
110, 164
Kessel, Albrecht von, Counselor at Ger-
man Embassy to the Holy See, 77
Kirkpatrick, Ivone, British Minister to
the Holy See, 86, 129
Kolbe, Maximilian, Franciscan priest in
Auschwitz, 25
Kubowitzki, Leo, Jewish spokesman, 6
Kulturkampf, 81, 84

L'Osservatore Romano, Vatican newspaper,
14; criticism of Soviet invasion of
Finland, 51, 169; protest against Ger-

(L'Osservatore Romano, continued)
man invasion of Low Countries, 52; as speaking for Pope, 61, 63; protest against deportation of Italian Jews, 63; on German concordat, 86; on German occupation of Rome and *razzia,* 144–45; protests against persecutions in France, 151

La Civiltà Cattolica, 30

LaFarge, John, SJ, American journalist, 128–29

Lang, Cosmo, Archbishop of Canterbury, 134

Lapide, Pinchas, Israeli diplomat and writer, 139

Lateran Accords, 38, 50, 75–77, 94, 141

Lau, Yisrael, Jewish spokesman, 7

Ledochowski, Wladimir, SJ, Jesuit General and director of Vatican Radio, 62

Lehnert, Pascalina, German nun in charge of papal household, 16; *Ich durfte ihm dienen: Erinnerungen an Papst Pius XII,* 31, 117; on Pope's personality, 127

Leo XIII, Pope, 92, 108

Levai, Jeno, historian, 165

Lewy, Guenter, historian, *The Catholic Church and Nazi Germany,* 35; on German Catholics, 99, 132–33

Lichtenberg, Bernhard, Dean (Propst) of St. Hedwig's Cathedral, Berlin, 25, 37, 166

Lieber, Robert, SJ, advisor to Pius XII, 16, 30; on German occupation of Rome, 59; on papal diplomacy, 107; on Pope's personality, 123, 126, 128

Lubac, Henri de, historian, on Bérard report, 151,

Lukacs, John, historian, 101

Lukas, Richard, historian, 74

Luxembourg, 52

Macmillan, Harold, British High Commissioner for Italy, on meeting Pius XII, 172

Maglione, Luigi, Vatican Secretary of State, on knowledge of Holocaust, 45; as spokesman for Pius XII, 65; letter to American bishops, 106; on Roman *razzia,* 143, 146; and Italian bishops, 148; on Bérard report,

150–51; on Polish protests, 156–57; on Romania, 163

Malachy, St., prophecies, 121

Marcone, Giuseppe, Apostolic Visitor to Croatia, 160, 162

Marrus, Michael, historian, 13, 36; on alleged anti-Semitism of Pius XII, 73; on Pope's German concerns, 99; on papal diplomacy, 111

Martini, Angelo, SJ, editor of Vatican documents, 29

Meir, Golda, President of Israel, 6

Menshausen, Fritz, German chargé at the Holy See, 64; as source on Pius XII's views, 105, 123–24

Mexico, 16

Miccoli, Giovanni, historian, *I dilemmi e i silenzio di Pio XII,* 35; on papal policy, 36–37; on inability of Pius XII to comprehend the Holocaust, 45n8; on Catholic anti-Semitism, 71–72; on papal diplomacy, 95

Michaelis, Meir, historian, *Mussolini and the Jews,* 73; on effect of public papal protest, 132; on Roman *razzia,* 144

Mindzenty, Josef, Cardinal Archbishop of Esztergom (Hungary), 21

Mit Brenender Sorge, see Pius XI

Monte Cassino, Abbey of, 21

Montini, Giovanni Battista, *see* Paul VI

Morley, John, historian, *Vatican Diplomacy and the Jews during the Holocaust,* 92, 135; on Croatia, 162; on Slovakia, 163–64; on Orsenigo, 168

Mortara Affair, 70–71

Mussolini, Benito, Italian dictator, 73, 94, 141; and security of Vatican, 76–77

Nathan, Joseph, Jewish spokesman, 5

Netherlands, 52

New York Times Magazine, 6

Nobécourt, Jacques, historian, 35–36

North Africa, British and American invasion of, 56

Nuremberg Laws, 70

Nuremberg Trials, 13

O'Carroll, Michael, historian, *Pius XII: Greatness Dishonoured,* 104; on Croatia, 160–61

Orsenigo, Cesare, nuncio to Germany, difficulties with Nazi regime, 68; on German Catholics, 101; not allowed to protest or visit Poland, 93, 154; as ineffective, 139, 168; congratulations to Hitler on escaping 1944 assassination attempt, 169

Orthodox Serbs in Croatia, 159–60, 161–62

Osborne, D'Arcy, British Minister to the Holy See, 30; as source of information to Vatican, 44; on Allied bombing of Germany, 65; on Allied bombing of Rome, 79; on Pius XII's personality, 126–27, 129; on German bombing of Britain, 170. *See also* Chadwick, Owen

Ossicini, Adriano, 73

Pacelli, Eugenio, *see* Pius XII

Pacelli family, 14

Papée, Kazimierz, Polish Ambassador to the Holy See, 30

Papeleux, Léon, historian, *Les silences de Pie XII,* 36, 170

Papen, Franz von, German diplomat, on concordat negotiations, 84–85

Paris, Edmond, historian, 161

Paul VI, Pope, (Giovanni Battista Montini), 29, 122; on Pius XII's alleged silence, 115; as Vatican subsecretary of state, on Bérard report, 150; on "rat line," 162

Pavelic, Ante, Croatian dictator, 20, 23, 159–62

Pawlikowski, John, historian, 8; on Pius XII's alleged anti-Semitism, 73; on need for more research, 178

Pétain, Marshal Henri Philippe, French President, 23; and Vichy French anti-Semitic laws, 149–51, 157

Petrusblatt, Berlin diocesan newspaper, 98

Phayer, Michael, historian, *The Catholic Church and the Holocaust, 1930–1965,* 34–35; on Pius XII and bishops, 37 n38, 41, 138, 167; on Pope's fear of destruction of Rome, 80; on Pope as mediator, 112; on Pope and Dutch Jews, 117n9; on Croatia, 118, 161; on Poles, 158; on "rat line," 162, 170–71;

on Hungary, 165; on Orsenigo, 168

Pius IX, Pope, 71, 92

Pius X, Pope, 92, 121, 122

Pius XI, Pope, 25, 121, 122, 128; and Eugenio Pacelli, 15, 16, 17; *Mit Brenender Sorge,* 17, 40, 42, 61, 88, 93, 97–98, 104, 133, 176; policy of concordats, 83–84; approval of Hitler's anti-Bolshevism, 84; and German concordat of 1933, 87, 98; and German Catholics, 97–98, 133; encyclicals: *Humani Generis Unitas,* 93; *Divini Redemptoris,* 104, 106

Pius XII, Pope (Eugenio Pacelli), aims and means, 36–41; Allied bombing of Germany, condemnation of, 169–70; anti-Semitism alleged, 70–75, 173; belief that a protest would make things worse, 114–20, 177; clergy, control of, 137–38; Cold War, views and actions on, 21, 94–96; Communism, fear of, 103–7, 175; Communists, condemnation of, 21, 24, 94–95, 96; critics charges against, 22–24; Croatia, relations with, 23, 159–63; death of, 21; diplomatic policy, 90–96, 175; early life, 14; election as pope, 17, 23; French Ambassador, response to June 1940 appointment of, 53; German bishops, relations with, 24, 165–67; German Catholics, views of, 97–102, 175–76; German concordat, negotiation of, 22, 82–88; protests against violations of, 88–89, 93; fear of German abrogation of, 174; German connections, 22–23; and Hitler, telegram to on occasion of 1939 assassination attempt, 169; Holocaust, knowledge of, 42–46; humanitarian work of papacy, 120, 168; Hungary, relations with, 23, 164–65; Italian bishops, relations with, 148; Italian Jews, order to shelter, 147–49; Italy under German occupation of, actions during, 20–21, 140–49; Jewish statements in support of at end of war, 5–6, 140; mediation of war attempts, 18, 108–113, 176–77; nuncio to Bavaria and Germany, 15–16, 34,

(Pius XII, Pope, continued)
72, 84, 103–4, 108, 137, 170; nuncios, control over, 138–39; papal rhetoric, 66–67; personality, 121–30; Poles, relations with, 153–58; private views, 63–66; public statements: to Belgian Ambassador (1939), to German pilgrims (1939), 48–49; to Polish pilgrims (1939), 49, 155; encyclical, *Summi Pontificatus* (1939), 28, 41, 49–51, 64, 93, 101, 109, 133, 155; Christmas message of 1939, 39, 51–52, 124; Easter homily (1940), 52; telegram to rulers of Belgium, the Netherlands, and Luxembourg (1940), 52; "Letter to French Church," (1940), 53; "Appeal to World for a Just Peace," (1940), 53; Christmas message of 1940, 53–54; Easter message of 1941, 54; address on feast of Sts. Peter and Paul (1941), 53–54; Christmas message of 1941, 55–56, 168; "Pleas to the Warring Nations" (1942), 56; Christmas message of 1942, 39, 46, 56, 57; patronal address (1943), 57–58, 114, 156; Christmas message of 1943, 58; patronal address (1944), 58–59; address on fifth anniversary of outbreak of war (1944), 59; Christmas message of 1944, 60; patronal address (June 1945), 60–61; addresses to Allied soldiers and German soldiers, 24, 59; "rat line," alleged support of, 24, 170–71; Roman Jews, reaction to September 1943 German ransom demand, 142; Roman *razzia*, October 1943, reaction to, 23–24, 142–47; Romania, relations with, 163; Rome, pleas against destruction of, 59, 79; Rome, concern over, 148, 174; secret negotiations agreement (1939–1940), 18, 95–96, 107, 109; Secretary of State of the Holy See, 16–17, 104; Slovakia, relations with, 23, 163–64; unconditional surrender doctrine, protests against, 59; United States Congress, talks to members of, 60; Vichy France, relations with, 23, 149–52; wartime problems, 18–21

Poland, and Poles, German attack on, 23, 52, 105; documents on, 30; Jews in, 42; papal statements on, 49–50, 58, 74; Vatican radio on, 62; and papal diplomacy, 93; Pius XII's views and actions toward, 153–58
Poliakov, Léon, historian, 24–25
Polish Corridor, 108, 154
Portugal, 78
Preysing, Konrad von, Bishop of Berlin, letters from Pius XII to, 115, 152, 155, 166–167, 168
Purdy, W. A., historian, 99

Raddatz, Fritz J., historian, 32
Radio Vatican, 61–62, 63, 151, 155
Radonski, Karol, Bishop of Wloclawek, 157
"rat line," 24, 162, 170–71
Reich Concordat of 1933, *see* Concordat of 1933
Reitlinger, Gerald, historian, 78
Repgen, Konrad, historian, 10, 87–89
Ribbentrop, Joachim von, German Foreign Minister, protests to Pius XII, 57, 65, 105, 124
Roeder, Felice, Bishop of Beauvais, 134
Roman Question, 15, 75
Roman *razzia* of October 1943, 23–24, 26, 142–47
Rome, Allied bombing of, and papal fears of destruction of, 21, 65, 79–80
Roosevelt, Franklin, President of the United States, 106, 175
Rotta, Angelo, nuncio to Hungary, 164
Rubenstein, Richard L., historian, 72
Rubinstein, William D., historian, 135–36
Ruhm von Oppen, Beate, historian, 37; on papal rhetoric, 66; on German Catholics, 101
Rychlak, Ronald, attorney, 5n

Sapieha, Adam, Archbishop of Cracow, 115; and papal protest, 156, 158
Scavizzi, Pirro, Italian chaplain, 116
Schioppa, Lorenzo, aide to nuncio, 72
Schneider, Burkhart, SJ, editor of Vatican documents, 29
Scholder, Klaus, historian, 83, 86–87

Senatra, Eduardo, journalist, 98–99

Seredi, Justinian, Cardinal Archbishop of Ezstergom (Hungary), 165

Sereny, Gitta, journalist-historian, 73

The Silence of Pius XII, see Falconi, Carlo

Slovakia, 23, 160

Soviet Union, 9; invasion of Finland, 18, 124; as occupying power, 49, 50, 54; fighting in Poland, 59, 60; invasion of Hungary (1956), 94–95

Soviet-German non-aggression pact of 1939, 18, 105

Soviet-Polish non-aggression pact of 1932, 52

Spain, 75, 78; Civil War, 16, 62, 104

Spanish Ambassador in Berlin, 105

Spartacist uprising in Germany, 81

Stalin, Josef, Soviet dictator, 170

Stalingrad, battle of, 56; German change of policy after, 158

Stepinac, Alojzije, Cardinal Archbishop of Zagreb, 21, 159, 161

Suhard, Emmanuel, Cardinal Archbishop of Paris, 152

Summi Pontificatus, see Pius XII

The Tablet, 115

Tardini, Domenico, Vatican undersecretary of state, 31, 88; letter to Sapieha, 115–16; on Pius XII's personality, 122–23, 128; and Bérard report, 150; answer to Poles, 157–58; on Tiso, 164

Tiso, Josef, President of Slovakia, 23, 163–64

Tisserant, Cardinal Eugène, 123, 149, 152–53

Tittmann, Harold, United States chargé at the Holy See, 45; and papal protest, 57, 102, 117

unconditional surrender doctrine, 48

United Jewish Appeal, aid to Pope, 19n

United States at war, 55, 56; Apostolic Delegate to, 106

Ustasha, persecutions, 19–20, 58, 159–63

Valeri, Valerio, nuncio to France, 149–51, 157

Van Hoek, Kees, journalist, 126

Vatican Council II, 2

Vatican Radio, *see* Radio Vatican

Versailles Treaty, 154

Vichy France, *see* France

Victor Emmanuel II, Italian King, 94

Wannsee conference, 20, 43

"We Remember: A Reflection on the Shoah," 5–8. *See also* Commission for Religious Relations with the Jews

Weimar regime, *see* Germany

Weiss, John, historian, 4

Weiszäcker, Ernst von, 30; German permanent undersecretary of state, 105–6; German Ambassador to the Holy See, 77–78, 79; on Pius XII's personality, 129; on October 1943 Roman *razzia*, 26, 27, 143–47

Wilhelm II, German Emperor, 15

Wills, Gary, historian, 128–29

Woodruff, Douglas, editor, 128

World Jewish Congress, 6, 165

World War I, propaganda, 44

Württemberg, 78

Wyszynski, Stefan, Cardinal Archbishop of Gniezo and Posen, 21

Yugoslavia, Communist government, 161

Zahn, Gordon, sociologist, *German Catholics and Hitler's Wars,* 99

Zevi, Tullia, Jewish spokesman, 7

Zuccotti, Susan, historian, *Under His Very Windows,* criticism of Pius XII, 34–35, 36, 177; on result of papal protest, 41, 74; on papal knowledge of Holocaust, 45; claims papal fear for Vatican, 75; on papal neutrality, 111; claims papal fear of retribution against Catholics, 118; on Jewish praise for Pius, 140; on Roman *razzia*, 143, 146; contends no papal order to help Italian Jews, 148–49

Pius XII and the Holocaust: Understanding the Controversy was designed and composed in Monotype Columbus by Kachergis Book Design, Pittsboro, North Carolina; and printed on 60-pound Writers Offset and bound by Thomson-Shore, Inc., Dexter, Michigan.